A Legal and Ethical Handbook for Ending Discrimination in the Workplace

A Legal and Ethical Handbook for Ending Discrimination in the Workplace

David A. Robinson

Paulist Press
New York/Mahwah, N.J.

Note: This book is an educational tool, not a substitute for consultation with a lawyer. If you need legal guidance as to a situation in your workplace, you should seek the advice of a lawyer in your locale and not simply rely on this book. There may be exceptions to some of the information contained in this book, depending on the state or states in which the employer and employee are located, the number of employees the employer has, and other factors. Also keep in mind that the laws discussed in this book, like all laws, could conceivably change in the future.

Cover design by Valerie Petro

Book design by Lynn Else

Library of Congress Cataloging-in-Publication Data

Robinson, David A., 1953–
    A legal and ethical handbook for ending discrimination in the workplace / by David A. Robinson
        p.   cm.
    Includes bibliographical references.
    ISBN 0-8091-4138-8 (alk. paper)
    1. Discrimination in employment—Prevention—Handbooks, manuals, etc.
2. Discrimination in employment—Law and legislation—Handbooks, manuals, etc. I. Title.
HD4903 .R55 2003
658.3'008—dc21

                                                                2003000733

Published by Paulist Press
997 Macarthur Boulevard
Mahwah, New Jersey 07430

www.paulistpress.com

Printed and bound in the United States of America

Contents

Preface

When I was a child in Longmeadow, Massachusetts, in the early 1960s, there was a kids' program on local TV called *The Ranger Andy Show*. Once a week, Ranger Andy would take out his banjo and sing a song called "You'll Find It in the Bible." He would find *biblical* guidance for virtually all of life's problems in that song. I loved that song. I would listen to it and then try to "find it in the Bible" when I needed answers to life's problems.

But as I grew into an adult, I began searching elsewhere for answers: psychology books, economics books, law books, and other "scholarly" sources. I didn't read the Bible for years. When I began writing this book—some forty years after I last heard "You'll Find It in the Bible"—I had no intention of putting religion in it. I am a lawyer, not a preacher.

Law can be boring to the average reader, though, so I decided to spice up the book with some quotations. I found good quotations in the Bible. Then I looked deeper into the Bible. I noticed that these quotations were not just "spice." They and their underlying stories were the milk, honey, and other basic ingredients of the recipe for ending discrimination in the workplace. The Bible contains much guidance on how employers can maintain a disciplined, productive workforce without discriminating against anyone and without constantly worrying about being sued by a disgruntled employee. The Bible also provides guidance to employ*ees* on how to achieve career success and not be victims of discrimination. Ranger Andy was right: "You'll find it in the Bible."

Of course, you'll also "find it" in law books, history books, anthropology books, and other scholarly sources. This book utilizes those sources as well. It is still more a "scholarly" book, particularly a *law* book, than a religion book. But the book finds congruence in all these sources on the subject of employer-employee relations.

The book concludes that if employers and employees will follow the Bible, they will follow the law. The laws against discrimination are based on biblical principles. By following these principles, employers and employees will end discrimination in the workplace.

David A. Robinson
Springfield, Massachusetts
March 31, 2003

Introduction

What This Book Is About

This book tries to end discrimination in the workplace by encouraging the offenders (employers who discriminate) *and* some of the victims (some of the employees who are, or feel, discriminated against) to *both* change their way of thinking.

By **discrimination,** we mean treating an employee less favorably due to his or her race, color, national origin, sex, age, disability, or religion. We also mean sexual harassment, which the law regards as a form of sex discrimination. Sexual-orientation discrimination (discrimination against gays and lesbians), which is illegal in thirteen states, will also be discussed.

The book will show that discrimination is forbidden not only by law but by the Bible. However, the Bible discourages lawsuits. "Do not sue the Brethren....It is already an utter failure for you that you go to law against one another," St. Paul told the Corinthians (1 Cor 6:1–7). "Avoid foolish disputes, genealogies, contentions, and strivings about the law; for they are unprofitable and useless," he told Titus (Titus 3:9).

How do we end discrimination without suing the offenders? The book argues that the proper way to end discrimination is through a *cooperative effort* by employers and employees. Most of the effort should come from employ*ers.* They should try harder to be color-blind, gender-blind, age-blind, religion-blind, and national origin–blind when dealing with their employees. But *some* of the effort should come from employ*ees.* If some employees will alter their behavior a bit, they will not be discriminated against. A cooperative effort will enable employers to avoid lawsuits and enable employees to avoid discrimination.

Most lawsuits by employees against employers are discrimination suits. Most "wrongful termination" suits—suits alleging that an employee was fired wrongfully, illegally, or unfairly—are discrimination suits. They allege that the employee's race, color, national origin, gender, age, disability, religion, or refusal to submit to the employer's sexual urgings is what motivated the employer to terminate the employee. There are other types of "wrongful termination" suits, such as "whistleblower" suits, "violation of public policy" suits, and "breach-of-contract" suits, but most wrongful termination suits allege race, color, national origin, sex, age, disability, or religion discrimination. That is because most employees, including the vast majority of employees who are not in unions and do not have written employment contracts with their employers, are employees "at will." They can be terminated at any time for any reason, except they cannot be terminated for an *illegal* reason. Race, color, national origin, sex, age, disability, and religion are *illegal* reasons. So to win a wrongful termination suit, they usually have to allege and prove they were fired because of their race, color, national origin, sex, age, disability, or religion.

Most books about employment discrimination try only to change how employ*ers* think. They lecture, scare, and cajole employers. "Don't discriminate!" "Discrimination is illegal, immoral, and bad for business." "Discrimination lawsuits are costly." "Diversity is good for business." Or they tell employers how to avoid getting caught: "Document everything the employee does wrong." "Don't say anything nice about the employee or he'll use it against you in court." But they say nothing to employ*ees*. This book tries to change the thinking of employers *and* employees who have discrimination problems, and tries to *inspire* rather than threaten and cajole them.

Why, you ask, should employ*ees* change? Employ*ees* aren't the ones breaking the law, employ*ers* are. Asking employ*ees* to change implies that employ*ees* are to blame for discrimination.

That's "blaming the victim." "Don't blame the victim," people say. "Blame the offender. Sue the offender!"

The problem with that is, lawsuits rarely accomplish much if anything. St. Paul said lawsuits are an "utter failure" (1 Cor 6:7) and "unprofitable and useless" (Titus 3:9). Jesus suggested that if someone does us wrong, we should "turn the other cheek" rather than sue (Matt 5:39). He also said, "Woe to you also, you lawyers! For you load men with burdens hard to bear and you yourselves do not touch the burdens with one of your fingers" (Luke 11:46).

Lawsuits are especially ineffective in employment discrimination cases. For nearly forty years (since the Civil Rights Act of 1964 was passed), lawsuits have been the main weapon in the fight against discrimination in the workplace. Yet there are still few women and people of color at the highest levels of American business.[1] There are more employment discrimination lawsuits today than there were ten, twenty, or thirty years ago. Relatively few employees who have sued have received much money or satisfaction in these suits (the news media report the occasional million-dollar winner but not the thousands of employees who sue and lose).[2] It is difficult for employees to prove they were fired (or not hired) "because of" or "as a result of" their race, color, national origin, gender, age, religion, or disability. Yet that is what they must prove in order to win the suit. And in most courts, they must convince at least 80 percent of the jurors (ten out of the twelve jurors) of it. If fewer than 80 percent are convinced of it, the employee loses (in most states).

Employment discrimination, like domestic violence and other offenses in which the victim spends many hours a day with the offender (sometimes for many years), often likes the offender, and is financially dependent on the offender, is not easily remedied by the legal system. The legal system works well in cases where the victim and the offender are strangers, not when the victim and offender have had a long, complicated relationship.

In fact, most employees who sue end up *worse off* financially than if they hadn't sued. Many have trouble landing new jobs. Many employers don't want to hire employees who sue employers. They don't want to be next. Employees who sue are unlikely to get good job references. Why should an employer say something nice about an employee who is suing (or threatening to sue) him? Such an employer will probably just say "no comment" or give minimal information.

Most of the progress for women and people of color has been in *government* employment, not private-sector employment. Our presidents (all white males) and governors (nearly all white males) have appointed women and people of color to high government positions. Nearly half of all cabinet officers, judges, and prosecutors today are women and people of color. Although many of them are outstanding, many others were appointed just to please certain voting groups (namely, women and people of color). White males need these groups' votes to get elected and reelected. Private-sector CEOs, on the other hand, are usually chosen by white males, not by women and people of color, and thus do not feel the same need to hire and promote women and people of color that presidents and governors do.

How can women and people of color make it to the top in American business? How can white males be persuaded to put women and people of color into top business positions? This book tells how.

The book is not just about law but also about history, economics, anthropology, and religion. The laws relating to labor and employment are derived from these sources. The term "master-servant relationship," which is the legal term for the employer-employee relationship in American law, comes from the Bible. "Exhort servants to be obedient to their own masters, to be well pleasing in all things, not answering back, not pilfering, but showing all good fidelity," said Paul to Titus (Titus

2:9–10). "Masters, give your servants what is just and fair, knowing that you also have a Master in heaven," Paul told the Colossians (Col 4:1). "Servants, be submissive to your masters with all fear, not only to the good and gentle, but also to the harsh," Peter told the Pilgrims (1 Pet 2:18).

Of course, employees don't like to be regarded as "servants." They find it demeaning. They should realize, however, that *everyone* who relies on others for a living is a "servant." That includes not only employees but also their bosses and company owners. It includes *self-employed* people. They all "serve" customers in one way or another. In return, the customers pay them money. The money provides a living for these employees, bosses, and self-employed people. Most of the *customers* are "servants," too. That is how they acquire the money to begin with. From the wealthiest business owner down to the poorest laborer, everyone who *works* is a "servant" of someone else. There is nothing demeaning about that.

The Bible is an excellent equal employment opportunity guide. This will surprise some people. Some people think the Bible *causes* discrimination. In fact, it has become fashionable in some circles to blame the Bible for race discrimination and sex discrimination. But the truth of the matter is, the Bible *forbids* discrimination in the workplace. The Bible tells employers how to run a "tight ship" (maintain a hardworking, disciplined workforce) while avoiding the troubled waters brought on by lawsuits. "He who sows sparingly will also reap sparingly, and he who sows bountifully will also reap bountifully," said Paul (2 Cor 9:6). That means employees should be hired, compensated, promoted, disciplined, and terminated based on *what their productivity and services are worth*, not on their race, color, national origin, gender, age, religion, or disability. It means employers need not put up with slothfulness, disobedience, or inability on the part of an employee just because the employee needs money to live on. An employer is not an employee's "keeper." The *Catechism of the Catholic Church* (pars. 2433–34) recommends that wages for employees take into account "the role and productivity of each, the state of the business, and the common good" as well as the monetary needs of the employee, and mandates that access to employment be open to all "without unjust discrimination."

Thus, employees who think they are victims of discrimination but who in fact are victims of their own slothfulness, disobedience, or inability will find little solace in the Bible or in court. The Bible urges employees to work hard and not blame their problems on their race, color, national origin, gender, age, religion, or disability unless their problems really are the result of discrimination.

Of course, the Bible is not "the law" in this country. This country separates "church" and "state" to a large extent.[3] But many of our laws are *derived* from the Bible. Our laws almost never *conflict* with the Bible. That is because our lawmakers (politicians) would be voted out of office by their constituents, most of whom worship the Bible or at least respect the moral teachings of the Bible, if a law were passed commanding people to do what the Bible forbids, or forbidding people to do what the Bible commands. Our employment discrimination laws, in particular, are consistent with the Bible. That should inspire employers to obey them.

"You" and "Your"

It is employ*ers*, more so than employ*ees*, who have to obey the discrimination laws. So when this book refers to "you" or "your," it generally means employ*ers*. However, employees can also benefit from following the advice.

Applicability

The rights of employers and employees depend in part on which of the fifty states they are in and how many employees the employer has. There are, to be sure, *federal* employment discrimination laws—which are the same in every state—but small employers (those with fewer than fifteen employees) are not governed by most of those federal laws. Larger employers (those with fifteen or more employees) are governed by those laws but not *only* by those laws. They are also governed by *state* employment discrimination laws. Some states' employment discrimination laws provide greater protection to employees than the federal laws do. And some states' employment discrimination laws govern *small* employers (employers with fewer than fifteen employees) as well as larger employers.

So it is impossible for a book on employment discrimination law to give advice that applies to all employers in all states in all situations. Even advice as simple as "Don't discriminate on the basis of gender, age, or religion" does not apply to all employers. Small employers in some states have the right to discriminate on the basis of gender, age, and religion if they want to. Statements about *federal* law, such as "the U.S. Supreme Court has made it more difficult for employees to prove they are 'disabled' under the Americans with Disabilities Act," have no relevance to employers, even large employers, in states that have disability discrimination laws that protect employees more than the Americans with Disabilities Act ("ADA") does.

That is why this is a short book. Very little can be said that is true for all employers in all states. This book tries to be applicable to as many employers as possible, but there may be occasional exceptions to its contents, depending on which state the employer is in and other unique circumstances of the particular employer. The book cannot address *all* the possible exceptions.

That is why, if you need legal advice about a particular situation, you should consult a lawyer in your state.

Law and Ethics

This book is more about law than ethics. Law can be "taught" more easily than ethics. Ethics are often "in the eye of the beholder." Two highly ethical people can have opposite opinions as to the same ethical question. That can also happen in law, but it happens less frequently in law. Two legal scholars can read the same law and have opposite opinions as to what the law requires. Think about the dispute over the 2000 presidential election. Both the Gore and Bush camps declared that the dispute should be decided by the "rule of law." But they had opposite opinions of what the "rule of law" was. The Gore camp said the law required a recount in Florida; the Bush camp said the law prohibited a recount in Florida. Worse yet, each camp's view of the law seemed to depend not so much on the wording of the law but on who they wanted to win!

And when the election was finally decided by a lawsuit *(Bush v. Gore)*, the U.S. Supreme Court did not make the "rule of law" much clearer, if at all. Four of the nine justices on the Court said the law requires a recount in Florida, while the other five said the law forbids a recount in Florida. If nine great legal minds can look at the same law and split 5-4 as to what the law requires, the legal system obviously has its limits as a way of resolving disputes.

That is why Jesus and St. Paul had little confidence in the legal system. The law is often "in the eye of the beholder."

But "ethics" is even more so. Here is an example. In early 2001 the Presbyterian Church of the U.S.A. had a feature on its Web site called "Ethics in the Workplace."[4] It asked this question: Is it ethical to fire a person who is close to retirement age in order to replace him with a younger employee who is willing to work for a lower salary?" An "ethicist" would probably say it is *not* ethical. An ethicist would say the employer should let the older employee finish his career with the company even though the company has to pay him more than it would pay a younger employee doing the same work (unless the younger worker can perform the job *better* than the older worker, in which case the ethicist might say it is ethical to fire the older worker). Some lawyers (not many, but some) might say it is not only unethical but also *illegal*. Those lawyers will argue that it is age discrimination.

But it is easy for ethicists, lawyers, and clergy to tell an employer what to do and how much to pay. The money is not coming from *them*. It is coming from the *employer*. So let's view the situation from the standpoint of the employer. Let's assume that the employer wants to be totally ethical and legal. Rather than immediately firing the older worker, the employer tells the older worker the facts and seeks input from the older worker as to what the ethical thing to do is. He tells the older worker that a qualified younger worker is seeking the older worker's job and is willing to do the job for a lower salary. The employer asks the older worker to respond. The older worker responds, "I'm going to talk to a lawyer."

The older worker talks to a lawyer. He also talks to an ethicist. The older worker, the lawyer, and the ethicist then arrange for a meeting with the employer. Let's call the older worker Oliver ("O" reminds you he is the older worker) and the others by their titles. Here is how their meeting goes:

Oliver: "Boss, I'd like you to meet my lawyer and ethicist."

Boss: "Hi."

Oliver's Lawyer: "I'm here to tell you that you can't fire Oliver. Firing him would be age discrimination. Age discrimination is illegal. You can't fire an older worker just because you'd prefer a younger worker."

Boss: "If I fire Oliver, it won't be because of his age; it will be because I found an employee who can do the job just as well as

Oliver for less pay. If Oliver were only twenty-five years old instead of sixty-four years old, I would fire Oliver if another prospect came along willing to work for less. So it has nothing to do with Oliver's age."

Oliver's Lawyer: "But the reason Oliver earns more is that he is older. Older workers tend to earn more."

Boss: "I talked to my lawyer. She said she thinks it is not age discrimination."

Ethicist: "But even if it isn't age discrimination, it still isn't right for you to fire Oliver. It is unethical. It is unethical to fire a longtime, dedicated employee just because someone else comes along willing to work for less. It is heartless and cruel. You're putting profits before people."

Boss: "Sir, where do you live?"

Ethicist: "I live in the ABC Apartment Building. I've lived there for many years."

Boss: "What do you pay for rent?"

Ethicist: "$600 a month."

Boss: "What if your lease were up and another apartment building offered you the same type of apartment in the same general location for $500 a month? Would you move?"

Ethicist: "I might. What does that have to do with anything?"

Boss: "You're saying you would 'fire' your longtime landlord just because someone offered you the same type of apartment for less. So why can't I fire a longtime employee like Oliver if someone offers to do his job for less?"

Ethicist: "You can't compare Oliver to a landlord. Oliver has feelings. He has needs. You need to be sensitive to that."

Boss: "Landlords are people, too. And they employ people. Wouldn't the people who work for your landlord be out of work if everyone were to move out like you would?"

Ethicist: "Sir, Oliver has been with you for many years, through thick and thin. He has been loyal to you. You owe him the dignity of letting him retire with your company."

Boss: "You have been with your landlord for many years, but that obviously means nothing to you. By the way, do you have a lease on your apartment?"

Ethicist: "Yes."

Boss: "Oliver has no 'lease' here. He does not have a two-year contract or a one-year contract. He has no contract. He is an 'employee at will.' He can quit whenever he wants, and I can fire him whenever I want."

Ethicist: "But he hasn't quit. He's been loyal to you."

Boss: "The only reason he hasn't quit is that he hasn't been able to find a job elsewhere that pays as much as he makes here. He would quit in a minute if he did. I paid him even when this company was struggling and I had no money to take home for myself. I paid him even when he was performing poorly due to his various personal problems. Yes, he's been loyal to me, but only because he had nowhere else to go. And I have been loyal to him. I owe him nothing. I've paid him every dime I owe him."

Ethicist: "Sir, what about Oliver's experience and maturity? Doesn't that count for something? It will take you a long time to train this younger worker and even then he will still be less experienced and mature than Oliver. Oliver can do a much better job than this younger worker. So you should pay Oliver more."

Boss: "I looked carefully into this younger worker's work history. He's young but he has solid work experience. He's very mature. He's much better with computers than Oliver is. Oliver likes to do things the old way. He still has trouble with spreadsheets. Oliver had the chance to take computer courses at company expense but wasn't interested. This younger worker will do just as good a job as Oliver, if not better. By the way, when does Oliver plan to retire?"

Oliver's Lawyer: "You can't ask that. It is illegal to ask an employee when he plans to retire. It is age discrimination. You cannot force an employee to retire at a certain age."[5]

Boss: "But what if he doesn't retire soon? What if he stays another ten years? Do I have to continue to pay him more than I'd have to pay someone else? That will add up to hundreds of thousands of dollars over the next ten years."

Oliver's Lawyer: "Okay, we'll tell you. Oliver plans to retire a year from today."

Boss: "Will you put that in writing?"

Oliver's Lawyer: "No. You have no right to ask for it in writing. You have no right to ask for it at all. You are on thin ice legally, sir."

Boss: "*I'm* on thin ice? *Oliver's job* is on thin ice!"

Oliver's Lawyer: "We'll sue."

Boss: "Even assuming that Oliver does plan to retire a year from today, what if he slacks off during the year? He knows he's about to retire. He has little incentive to do a good job. What if he gets lazy? Can I fire him?"

Oliver's Lawyer: "We'll cross that bridge when we come to it."

(Notice that one person at this meeting has not yet spoken: Oliver. Finally he speaks.)

Oliver: "I don't want to sue. I just want to keep my job."

Boss: "Make me an offer."

Oliver: "Huh?"

Boss: "Try to persuade me to keep you. Try to explain to me why it makes good business sense for me to keep you. Your lawyer and ethicist have just about persuaded me to fire you. You have not yet spoken. Speak."

Oliver: "What salary is this younger person willing to accept?"

Boss: "$40,000."

Oliver: "You are paying me $60,000. How about if I agree to a cut in salary to $50,000? May I stay?"

Boss (pondering for a few seconds, then deciding): "Yes. But you must continue to do a good job. If you get lazy, I can still fire you."

Oliver: "Okay. You've got a deal."

(Everyone shakes hands.)

Boss: "Oh, one more thing. A few days ago one of our suppliers told me she is looking for someone to run a new department at her company. She's looking for someone mature, with lots of experience. The job starts next month. Maybe she'd be interested in you."

Oliver: "What does the job pay?

Boss: "I think she said $85,000 a year."

Oliver (ecstatic): "I've always wanted to work there. I'm going to apply. Thanks for telling me."

Boss: "Wait a minute. I thought we had a deal. You just agreed to work for me for the next year for $50,000, then retire.

Oliver (to his lawyer): "Am I stuck with that deal?"

This scenario teaches us much about law and ethics. First, law is not always clear. A few courts have held that it is age discrimination to fire an older worker in order to replace him with a younger worker for lower pay, but most courts have held it is not. This is one reason many employees who sue often end up with no job and no case: The law is not always clear.

Second, ethics are even less clear. They are particularly unclear when the spotlight is only on *one* of the disputants. The Presbyterian Church's ethical question focuses only on the *boss's* ethics. What about *Oliver's* ethics? The ethically correct course for the boss depends in part on Oliver's ethics.

Third, discrimination is often unclear. Oliver thinks he is a victim of discrimination, but his boss thinks Oliver is a victim of Oliver's own failure to take computer courses. The boss gave Oliver the opportunity to upgrade his computer skills and be competitive with workers who already have good computer skills, but

Oliver declined the opportunity. In the boss's view, the younger applicant is more qualified by reason of his computer skills, not his age. The boss claims age has nothing to do with it. Who will the jury believe, Oliver or the boss? That is anyone's guess.

Fourth, we should not condemn an employer's ethics without knowing all the facts. You probably thought the ethical question was an easy one at first. Your initial "judgment" was probably that it would be unethical to fire Oliver. But as you learned more and more facts, maybe you changed your mind. In any event, you should not judge the ethics of an employer until you have tried to stand in that employer's shoes. Nor should you judge an employer's ethics without examining what *you* would do if you were the employ*ee* in that situation. Would *you* quit and take the $85,000-a-year job at the other company? If it is ethically okay for you to *quit* a job in order to make more money elsewhere, why isn't it ethically okay for your boss to *terminate* you so that *he* can make more money? The boss can make more money by hiring someone to do your job for a lower salary. If you can put *your* "profits" first, why can't the boss put *his* "profits" first?

Maybe it is better not to judge at all. "Judge not, that you be not judged," Jesus said (Matt 7:1–2). "For with what judgment you judge, you will be judged; and with the same measure you use, it will be measured back to you."

Fifth, litigation should be a last resort. Oliver achieved more by negotiating with his boss than he would have by suing his boss: he kept his job. He took a pay cut, but in his case that was better than getting fired. He might have had difficulty finding a $50,000 job elsewhere. Maybe he'll be hired for the $85,000 job, but maybe not. If he is hired for it, the boss won't mind. The boss will be glad to see Oliver leave. The boss will then hire the younger worker for $40,000. Best of all, there's no lawsuit!

That is why this book focuses not only on what employ*ers* can do, but also on what employ*ees* can do to end discrimination.

A *combined* effort is the best way to end it. Fighting one another in a lawsuit hurts *both*. The employee rarely wins, and the employer never wins. For, even when the employer wins *the suit*, the employer *loses* the time, effort, and money expended in defending against the suit.

And even though ethics lies "in the eye of the beholder," it is possible to offer ethical guidance. The Presbyterian Church recommends that you ask yourself the following questions when confronted with an ethical dilemma in the workplace:

> 1. Will my actions show unconditional love to the others involved in the situation?
>
> 2. Are there specific biblical teachings that apply to this situation? If not, how can I apply my knowledge of God's Word and Christ's example to this specific dilemma?
>
> 3. What answer does my own conscience tell me will bring me inner peace, even though it also may be painful?
>
> 4. What faith example will I provide to my coworkers and my family by the decision I make?[6]

If you keep those questions in mind as you read this book, you will be better able to make employment decisions that are legally and ethically sound.

Chapter One
Ending Race Discrimination

"He has made from one blood every nation of men to dwell on all the face of the earth." Acts 17:26

"Racial superiority is a mere pigment of the imagination." Dr. Laurence J. Peter (author of *The Peter Principle.*[7])

Your Employees Are All the Same Race: The Human Race

Be color-blind. That is the best way to end race discrimination. It is the best way to prevent race discrimination lawsuits. Ignore race and skin color completely (except in two or three situations that will be discussed below). You should not even mention race or skin color in the workplace unless you absolutely have to.

If you are a boss and you enjoy friendly, constructive, well-intentioned discussions about race and culture, that is wonderful; but try, if at all possible, to do it *outside* the workplace and with people who are *not* your employees. The book will have more to say about diversity training, affirmative action, and multiculturalism later in this chapter.

(This book uses the words *race* and *color* interchangeably. Although the two words occasionally have different meanings in the employment discrimination context, they usually have the same meaning. So when we say race, we also mean color; and when we say color, we also mean race.)

Some people don't want employers to be color-blind. They want employers to notice and think about race and color all the time. They want racial and cultural diversity "celebrated" in the workplace. They want an employer to excuse an employee's chronic lateness if that employee is from a "culture" where being late is a "sign of respect." Or they want *reverse* discrimination: They want you to hire a less-qualified job applicant of a certain race over a more-qualified job applicant of another race just to achieve racial diversity and to correct past discrimination (they assume that all white-owned workplaces committed race discrimination in the past). Or they say color-blindness is impossible. "As long as people have eyes, they won't be color-blind," they say.

They may be right, for all we know. But *they* are not *the law*. *The law* generally requires you to be color-blind when dealing with your employees.[8] Being color-blind significantly reduces your risk of being sued for race discrimination. Whether color-blindness is the right way or the wrong way to deal with employees does not matter. Even if it is the wrong way, it is *the law*. You should obey the law even if you think the law is wrong. St. Peter said, "Submit yourselves to every ordinance of man for the Lord's sake" (1 Pet 2:13). You can try to *change* the law through the political process if you think the law is wrong, but *until* the law is changed, you should *obey* it.

The Bible commands us to be color-blind: "God created man in His own image...male and female" (Gen 1:27).[9] That means that *all* human beings, regardless of race or color, are created in God's image. It means all races and colors of humans are equally close to God. It means you should not treat one race better than another. "He has made from one blood every nation of men to dwell on all the face of the earth" (Acts 17:26).

The Reverend Dr. Martin Luther King, Jr.'s goal was a color-blind society. "I have a dream that my four little children will one day live in a nation where they will not be judged by the color of their skin but by the content of their character," he said in his "I Have a Dream" speech.

How to Be Color-Blind

Here are some suggestions to help you become color-blind. They are mental exercises to help you rid yourself of racist thoughts (if you have any). If you have no racist thoughts, you can skip ahead to page 26.

But if you are one of those people who believe that some races are smarter or better than others, here are some suggestions:

First, always keep in mind one very important fact, a fact that many people do not realize: *skin color is just a sunscreen.* It has nothing to do with brainpower. Dark skin means that a person's distant ancestors were from a part of the world where it is sunny and hot most of the time, such as Africa or other places near the Earth's equator. Dark skin was nature's way of protecting them from the sun's rays. Light skin means one's distant ancestors were from colder, less-sunny climates such as Scandinavia, Ireland, England, Germany, France, Poland, and Russia, and did not need such sun protection. Always keep in mind the following superb analysis that appeared in a *New Haven Register* article about race:

> *Homo sapiens* [human beings] originated in Eastern Africa about 200,000 years ago. Then, about 100,000 years ago, a group of this original population of modern humans left Africa and spread out among the world.
>
> [A]ll early modern humans probably appeared similar to populations in Africa, and then adapted to the different environments in which they settled.
>
> "If you look at an ultraviolet map of the world, it correlates with human skin color," said [Nicholas] Bellantoni [a University of Connecticut anthropology professor].
>
> Skin with sun-blocking dark pigment is a significant advantage to people in extremely sunny climates. However, people who settled in Northern Europe

received less benefit from skin pigment, which they slowly lost.[10]

Skin color is thus a function of *climate*, not *brainpower.* As the *Catechism of the Catholic Church* (par. 1934) states, "All men have the same nature and the same origin." As the Lutheran Church-Missouri Synod's statement "Racism: A Christian Response" notes, "God created out of one man all members of the human family....Any and all attempts to identify certain people or groups as somehow lesser members of humankind are therefore a blasphemous affront to our Creator."[11]

Keep that in mind, and you will liberate yourself from prejudice.

You might also want to try this: suppose God is black. "Suppose God is Black" was the title of an August 23, 1966, *Look* Magazine cover story by Senator Robert F. Kennedy. "But suppose God is black," Kennedy wrote. "What if we go to Heaven and we, all our lives, have treated the Negro as an inferior, and God is there, and we look up and he is not white? What then is our response?"[12] That's a good question. A *great* question.

Some Bible scholars might argue that God cannot possibly be black. His Son was (is?) Jewish and nearly all Jews are *white*, they'll point out. But here is the weakness in their argument: All races think God looks *just like them.* Whites think God is white, blacks think God is black (many think Jesus was/is black), and Asians think God is Asian (the March 27, 2000, issue of *Newsweek,* p. 58, showed a Hindu painting of Jesus, depicting him as brown). For that matter, *men* think God and Jesus are men but some women (not many women, but some women) have begun to envision God and Jesus as androgynous (male-female hybrids). As Pope John Paul II observed, "Christ is the medium through which we see the face of God."[13] No wonder many people envision

Christ as they envision themselves. This prompts cynics to wonder, is man the creation of God, or God the creation of man?

Biblical accounts of God, even if *inspired* by God, were *written* by men, not by God. These men knew only their own race. They did not have television, the Internet, encyclopedias, or airplanes to enable them to see people from other parts of the world. The Bible was written in and around ancient Palestine, so it stands to reason that the men who wrote it thought God looked like the predominantly Caucasian population (Jewish, Arab, Greek, and Roman) in and around Palestine. They had never seen the people of China or central Africa, who look different.

The Bible does not say what race God is. To the extent that the Bible says anything at all about race, it regards the races as *equal*. This makes sense because the number of white people and black people in the world is roughly equal. The number of Asians is even greater. We should all keep that in mind and treat the races equally.

Some people think God intended the races to be separate: whites in Europe, blacks in Africa, Asians in Asia. But as the above analysis suggests, it is the opposite: God intended humans to spread out around the world and become whatever skin color best suited them to the climate. That may explain *why* the Bible was written in the Middle East: It is where Europe, Africa, and Asia all meet. That is a sign that God is equally close to all three races. Each human being should regard the races as equal.

Those who believe that God intended whites and blacks to live separately should keep in mind that *blacks* are not the ones who violated God's "plan." *Whites* are. Whites captured (or "purchased") blacks in Africa and brought them to America to live among and serve the white population. Whites must "do the right thing" and make sure that blacks have the same rights and opportunities whites have.

The same holds true regarding the Puerto Rican population. Like the black population, the Puerto Rican population did not *ask* to become U.S. citizens. They were *forced* to become U.S. citizens (many whites do not even know that Puerto Ricans are U.S. citizens). The United States wanted to control Puerto Rico so that no other nation (such as the former Soviet Union, which eventually gained a foothold in nearby Cuba) would. So the United States took control of Puerto Rico and made Puerto Ricans U.S. citizens. The United States must do the right thing and treat Puerto Ricans the same as white Americans.

Here are some more tips. First, don't "accentuate the negative." One element of racist thinking is to notice the race of a person only when the person does something *bad* or *stupid* but not notice it when the person does something *good* or *smart*. If a black person lets a white person cut in line in front of him in stalled traffic, the white person appreciates that, but the fact that this good person is black does not always register in the white person's mind. However, if the black person had *not* let the white person cut in, the white person would most likely have noticed that the "inconsiderate" person is black. If a white person is given the correct change by ten consecutive black store clerks but is given the wrong change by the eleventh one, the white person subconsciously (or maybe even consciously) thinks, "dumb black person." It probably did not occur to this white person that three of the last ten *white* store clerks also gave him the wrong change.

Second, don't judge the intelligence of the black population by their scores on standardized tests in school. Blacks tend, on average, to score lower on SATs and IQ tests than whites and Asians do. Does that mean they are less intelligent than whites and Asians? No. Does it mean their schools are inferior? Probably not. It means that blacks (not *all* blacks, but many blacks) don't like taking these tests.[14] Many blacks don't try their hardest on these tests. Why? Because they don't like being "tested" by whites, especially for no reason. Blacks enjoy school as much as whites and Asians do,[15] and learn as much in

school as whites and Asians do. But blacks are more likely to differentiate "testing" from schooling. They don't like being tested just
for the sake of being tested.[16] The purpose of an IQ test or SAT is
not to educate but to...*test*. Many blacks find it demeaning to be
"tested" or "ranked" in school, especially when the tests and rank-
ings are administered by *whites*. Being oppressed is bad enough.
Being "tested" or "ranked" by the oppressor is even worse.

Employment tests are different. They are for the purpose of
hiring. They help determine whether someone will earn a living.
They really count! Blacks should have the same incentive to do
well on employment tests as whites do. Consequently, it is okay
for employers to hold black job applicants to the same standards
as white job applicants when it comes to *employment* testing, so
long as the tests are fair and not racially biased.

One could argue, of course, that the SAT is an "employment
test" because it determines whether someone goes to college and
thus whether someone eventually gets a good job. But that is not
quite true. The SAT determines *which* college someone attends
more than it does *whether* someone attends college. Even students
with low SAT scores are usually admitted to some college. A significant number of students who score above average on the SAT are
no smarter than the ones who score below average, but they are
more *status-conscious* and want to go to a *prestigious* college more
than the below-average scorers do. So they try harder when preparing for and taking the SAT than the below-average scorers do.[17]

The United Methodist Church's General Commission on
Religion and Race offers two good tips for improving race relations: (1) don't feel threatened when interacting with persons of
races different from your own, and (2) seek to befriend persons
from racial and ethnic groups other than your own.[18]

Hopefully these suggestions and mental exercises will help
eliminate whatever tendency you might have to "accentuate the
negative." Not everyone has this tendency, but some people do.

Exceptions

For most employers, there are only two exceptions to the advice "Be color-blind." One is when you have two job applicants, one white and one black, who are *equally* qualified. If your company is overwhelmingly white, you should opt for diversity and hire the black applicant. In addition to the other benefits of diversity (it's good for business), diversity will help you if you or your company are ever sued for race discrimination by a black employee. An overwhelmingly white workforce—or even just an overwhelmingly white upper echelon within a company—will look suspicious to the EEOC (Equal Employment Opportunity Commission), a judge, or a jury, particularly if you are located in an urban area with a sizeable black population. Although your workforce is not *required* to reflect the demographic percentages that exist in your community, a diverse workforce does tend to show that you do not discriminate against people of color.

But if the two applicants are *not* equally qualified, you should hire the *better*-qualified applicant—the applicant who, based on your objective appraisal of everything you know about him or her, you think would do the job better—whatever color that applicant happens to be. This definition of "better qualified" is, however, flexible. It gives you some leeway. For example, if you wish to attract black customers, perhaps you should try harder to hire black employees. If you have two applicants, one white and one black, and it is a *very close call* which of them is better qualified, you probably can and should choose the black applicant. This is appropriate *affirmative action.* (Never do the opposite: hire a white person over an equally qualified black person just to please white customers or white employees.)

What is *in*appropriate affirmative action (and illegal discrimination) is hiring a black person over a white person even though the white person is, by any objective standard, better qualified.

There is an increasing number of reverse-discrimination cases: whites suing employers and educational institutions for hiring or admitting blacks who were less qualified than these white applicants.[19] Many whites are winning these cases.

The second exception comes into play if you have terminated a black employee. You then should consider hiring a black person to replace him or her. It is difficult (not impossible, but difficult) for a terminated black employee to claim that the employer is prejudiced against blacks if the employer replaced that employee with a black person.

For some employers, another exception may apply if they are operating under consent decrees or some types of government contracting requirements mandating them to hire more people of color.

Another "exception," of sorts, applies if the government *asks* you to count and report how many women and people of color you employ. Some employers are *required* to do this, including most employers with one hundred or more employees. Ordinarily, you can count them visually; you do not have to ask each employee. This is not really "considering" race or gender. It is just counting and reporting.

Affirmative Action (Is Not the Same as "Reverse Discrimination")

The mere fact that an employer has chosen, or is required, to be an "affirmative action" employer does not mean the employer can, or must, hire less-qualified people of color over better-qualified white employees. *Affirmative action* is a highly misunderstood term. Some think it means "reverse discrimination": hiring a less-qualified job applicant over a more-qualified applicant just because the less-qualified applicant belongs to an historically oppressed or underrepresented group, such as an ethnic minority or the female gender. Many whites and males are adamantly opposed to reverse discrimination.

But the true meaning of affirmative action is simply taking extra steps to ensure that women and minority-group members know about your job openings and feel welcome in your workplace. Affirmative action of this latter type is perfectly legal, proper, and advisable. It "seeks to befriend" persons from racial and ethnic groups other than your own (to borrow the words of the United Methodist Church a few pages ago) but does not give preference to one race over another. Keep in mind that the workforce is not becoming whiter, younger, or more male. It is becoming more female, racially diverse, and older. Diversity is good. Do not, however, hire or retain unqualified, incompetent, or insubordinate people of color just to look diverse. No law (no law we are aware of, anyway) requires you to maintain, or even try to maintain, the same demographics in your workplace as exist in your community or neighborhood (although there may occasionally be a government contract with which your company or organization has some involvement that might require you to have a certain percentage of minority workers; the constitutionality of such contracts is frequently litigated, and the law occasionally changes in this regard). However, the more your workplace does reflect those demographics, the harder it is for anyone to accuse you of racism.

Diversity Training?

This book neither encourages nor discourages "diversity training." Some diversity trainers are helpful. Others are counterproductive. If you bring in a diversity trainer, make sure you do not express any negative, prejudicial or stereotypical feelings about any group—even if you have such feelings—during training or at any other time. The less you say about race in the workplace, the better. Let the diversity trainer do most if not all the talking.

Any such talk on your part can be used against you in court to prove that you are "racist" or "prejudiced." Diversity training is more desirable if done for the purpose of preparing employees to do business in *foreign countries.*

Avoid the words "culture" and "multiculturalism." People who use those words are usually talking about *race* and *color* but think "culture" and "multiculturalism" are more "politically correct." Increasingly, the word "culture" is being used to sugar-coat old stereotypes and overgeneralizations. It nearly always means something *other than* culture. If not race or color, then language, national origin, gender, geography, religion, economic class, sexual orientation, or something else. One time at a roundtable discussion, a black person said to a white person whom he had never met, "You and I come from different cultures. We have different ways of communicating."

The white person responded, "What culture do I come from?"

The black person said, "I don't know."

The white person asked, "Then how do you know I come from a different culture than you do?"

The black person answered, "Because you are white."

The white person said, "Then what you mean is, I am of a different *race* than you. I'll concede that I am of a different race than you. But race is not the same as culture. You don't know whether I am rich or poor, what I do for a living, what time I eat or go to bed. You know absolutely nothing about me except my race."

"Culture" and "multiculturalism" are also used to justify comments like, "Germans are very punctual but Italians tend to be late; it's their culture." "That is part of the male culture." "It's the corporate culture." "People in New York eat dinner late; that is their culture." "Asians do not like to make eye contact; it is against their culture." Korean culture is this or that. Puerto

Ricans like this or that. Irish, Jews, Southerners, Northerners, whatever.

Ignore such generalizations. People are people. Some Germans are punctual and some are late. Some New Yorkers eat dinner late, others eat early. To the extent that people think or communicate differently from one another, it has nothing to do with their race, color, gender, age, ability/disability, or religion. Someone can be your exact age, ethnicity, profession, gender, religion, economic background, and live on your street, but you will not necessarily like him or agree with him on anything. Conversely, someone different from you racially, religiously, professionally, economically, and in every other "cultural" way might be a close friend of yours. In the workplace, the less you think about and talk about race, skin color, national origin, gender, religion, age, disability, and "culture," the better.

Summary

This discussion ("Be color-blind") boils down to the following simple advice:

• When firing, laying off, demoting, or disciplining employees, or when setting pay or other terms of employment, be totally color-blind. In other words, when taking *negative* or *neutral* action, be color-blind.

• When recruiting, hiring, or promoting employees, be color-blind except when the qualifications of black and white candidates are *equal* or *very close* (too close to call), in which case you should opt for diversity: Hire the black candidate, especially if you have a shortage of black employees at that particular job level. In other words, when taking *positive* action, you may wish to consider color.

• Do not talk about race or racial differences except when truly necessary.

Chapter Two
Ending Gender Discrimination

"She considers a field and buys it; from her profits she plants a vine-yard. She girds herself with strength, and strengthens her arms. She perceives that her merchandise is good." Proverbs 31:16–18

Treat Men and Women the Same
(Except in Regard to Pregnancy,
Manner of Dress, and Restrooms)

Try not to differentiate in any way between men and women in the workplace. Besides referring to a male as "he" or "Mr." and a female as "she" or "Ms." (or, if she prefers, "Miss" or "Mrs."), and besides providing separate restrooms and allowing men and women to dress differently, try to pretend that everyone is of the same gender—the "worker" gender. The law says you should treat women and men the same unless the woman is pregnant and close to giving birth or has just given birth (in which case she has some rights men don't have), or if there is a job that can only be performed by one gender. For example, if you need someone to model women's clothes, you can restrict your hiring to women for that position. That is called a "bona fide occupational qualification," or "BFOQ." Use gender-neutral language in oral and written communication. Don't call women over the age of eighteen "girls."

This advice to treat men and women the same might upset some women (of course, it might also upset some men). After years of trying—successfully—to prove that men and women have *equal* abilities (except perhaps that men have more upper-body strength), some women (and some men) are now saying that women *think*, *communicate*, and *manage employees* differently than men do.

Employers should ignore such talk. For thousands of years, one major cause of discrimination against women was the belief that women think differently than men. That belief resulted in women earning less than men and being subordinate to men in many types of employment. In the 1970s and '80s, women rejected that belief. As a result, women made great strides toward achieving full equality with men in the workplace. Today, however, that belief is back in vogue.

Keep in mind, however, that that belief—the belief that women think, communicate, and manage employees differently than men do—is held and expressed mainly by *authors*, *lecturers*, and *college professors*, not managers. *Managers* should *not* hold or express that belief. Managers who express that belief or base their managerial decisions on that belief risk being sued for sex discrimination.

If you are a manager, you should *ignore* all statements and literature that argue that women think, communicate, or manage differently than men do. Such arguments are generalizations that ignore the fact that not all men are the same and not all women are the same. Moreover, these generalizations are usually based on immeasurable characteristics and anecdotal observations. These generalizations are nothing new. They are as old as time. They have historically hurt women more than helped women in the quest for equality. Examples of such generalizations are: "Women use their instincts and emotional intelligence more than men do. Men just use logic." "Women prefer working in groups; men prefer working alone." "Women are less assertive than men." "Women are more nurturing than men." "Women are better communicators than men are." "Men don't ask directions." "Men don't cry." "Men can only think about one thing at a time; women can think about many things at a time." "Women think 'outside the box' better than men do."

The people who make such statements mean well. They are trying to empower women. But in fact they are doing the opposite. They are perpetuating old stereotypes about women, such as the stereotype that men prefer logic to instinct. Remember the old stereotype of a woman complaining to her husband, "I hate it when you're logical"? These people are claiming that that is absolutely true: Men are too logical. "Men should use less logic and more feelings and intuition, like women do," these people say. Such statements lead to legal trouble. If a *male manager* were to make such statements, he would be accused of "degrading" and "devaluing" women. He might get sued for sex discrimination. He would be a dead duck in court.

You should *treat men and women the same* and *not talk about gender differences at all*.

Women managers who talk about how women are better at one thing or another than men are (such as having better "intuition," "listening skills," or "communication skills" than men have) risk being sued for sex discrimination by male subordinates and rejected male job applicants. They might even be sued for creating a "hostile work environment" toward men. Women should avoid such talk. Such talk will cause men to file sex discrimination lawsuits.

Men and Women Are Both from Earth[20]

Employers should reject all generalizations that men are this and women are that. Such generalizations are no different than generalizations claiming that white people are this and black people are that. Such generalizations only lead to trouble. Such generalizations come dangerously close to saying, "Women are better than men" or "Men are smarter than women." That is no different from saying, "Blacks are better than whites" or "Whites are smarter than blacks" or some other rash, racist, sexist generalization. It is dangerous stuff. As Carol Gilligan warned in her famous book on male-female psychological differences, *In a Different Voice: Psychological Theory and Women's Development*, "…it is difficult to say 'different' without saying 'better' or 'worse.'"[21]

You should not assume anything about a person's thinking just because of his or her gender, race, color, national origin, age, disability, or religion. Many blacks are smarter than many whites, many whites are smarter than many blacks, many men are smarter than many women, and many women are smarter than many men. That is all we know. That does not tell us anything about a *particular* black person, white person, male, or female. Don't lump people together just because they are the same gender, race, color, age, national origin, ability/disability, or religion. Regard each person as an *individual* who may be very different from other people of his or her gender, race, color, national origin, age, ability/disability, or religion.

Be skeptical of the "studies" these people mention. There are all kinds of "studies" showing differences between men and women, whites and blacks, and other groups. Hitler relied on such "studies." All racist, sexist thinkers rely on such studies. That is because such "studies"—especially the ones based on IQ tests and combined SAT scores—tend to make white males look smarter than women (in math and science, anyway) and blacks. For every "study" showing that women have some advantage over men, there is a study, or test scores, showing that men have some advantage over women. "In One Ear, Without the Other" was a November 2000, newspaper headline[22] about a study showing that men listen with the left side of their brains while women listen with both sides of their brains. The first line of the article read, "Score one for exasperated women: New research suggests men really do listen with just half their brains." Numerous women, and some men, went on talk shows and said this study proves once and for all that men "just don't listen." But men countered by saying that in reality the study shows that men *have more brainpower* than women: Men need only *half* their brains to hear as much as women hear with their *whole* brains.

Employers should ignore such studies and debates. They only lead to feuds and discrimination. They create friction rather than unity. There are studies showing that certain ethnic groups have more athletic ability or mathematical ability than other ethnic groups. "Study finds ethnic link to math test scores," was an April 2001 headline.[23] Whether there is or is not a link between ethnicity and math scores, and whether that link, if it exists, is due to one factor or another factor, should be of no concern to employers. Employers who rely on such studies and let these studies guide their behavior at work are asking for trouble—*legal* trouble. *Big* legal trouble. Employers should disregard all studies, books, seminars, and discussions that show intellectual or emotional differences between men and women, whites and people of color, old people and young people, etc.

Employers should also disregard statements to the effect that men were "brought up" one way and women the other way. Some men were, some weren't. Some women were, some weren't. Furthermore, not every man and woman does what they were "brought up" to do. A common generalization about men, for example, is that they don't cry. They were "brought up" to stifle their emotions rather than cry. But is this generalization true? Consider this April 19, 2001, *Boston Globe* headline: "Cowboys Shed Tears As Stock Yard Ends Era."[24] When the Union Stock Yards in San Antonio, Texas, closed in 2001 after 112 years in business, "Hardscrabble Texas cowboys wept as the final gavel fell," according to the article.

So much for generalizations. Not only do *ordinary* men cry, *ultimate* men—*cowboys*—cry.

In short, employers should *disregard all generalizations about men and all generalizations about women.* Generalizing is stereotyping, and stereotyping leads to discrimination. The more you discriminate or differentiate between men and women or between one race and another race, the more legal trouble you potentially bring upon yourself. You should not differentiate between men and women (except in the three aspects listed above—dress codes, restrooms, and maternity leave—and one other aspect we will mention at the end of this chapter) or between whites and people of color. To "differentiate" is basically to *discriminate,* and *discrimination* is usually *against* a group, or *in favor* of one group at the *expense* of another group.

If college professors wish to conduct experiments to see if men think differently than women, fine. If teachers and trainers want to help people learn to value or even just tolerate diversity, that too is fine. Everyone should value or at least tolerate diversity. In your *behavior,* however—at least in the workplace—you should *treat men and women the same.*

That is what lawyers who represent women in sex discrimination cases tell juries. The lawyer for a woman professor who was awarded $12 million by a jury in a sex discrimination suit against a college said, "We asked the jury to send a message that it is not appropriate to treat women differently than men."[25] Her lawyer was correct. As a general rule, it is not appropriate to treat women differently than men in the workplace. Differential treatment can lead to legal trouble.

For all these reasons, this book recommends against diversity training that deals with gender (or religion or sexual orientation, for that matter). Perhaps if you have some employees who do business in certain foreign countries where, by law, women are treated differently than men, those employees might benefit from such training as it relates to those countries.

Some men (and some women) believe that equality for women in the workplace conflicts with the Bible, or with nature. They are mistaken. They base their belief on biblical passages that they believe give husbands more authority than wives *in the home*. But regardless of whether their interpretation of those passages is correct or incorrect, those passages do *not* give men more authority than women *in the workplace*. Even the Southern Baptist Convention, which issued a policy statement in 2000 declaring that wives should "graciously submit" to their husbands, does not advocate or tolerate sex discrimination in the *workplace*.

God designed us so that only women get pregnant and nurse babies, which leads some men (and some women) to believe that women were designed to stay home with children while men go out to work. But remember, God also gave men and women the same brainpower, brainpower that has created a modern world that values thinking more than brawn. Thus it is perfectly natural for women in modern times to work outside the home just as men do. Of course, as the proverb at the top of this chapter indicates, it was perfectly natural in biblical times as well.

Indeed, Catholic schools and hospitals have been run by women for centuries (including direct supervision over doctors). The United Methodist Church has declared, "We affirm women and men to be equal in every aspect of their common life. We therefore urge that every effort be made to eliminate sex-role stereotypes in activity and portrayal of family life. We affirm the right of women to equal treatment in employment, responsibility, promotion, and compensation."[26] The Presbyterian Church U.S.A. advocates "full inclusiveness and equality [between men and women] in the church and in society."[27]

As for brawn, few jobs require such upper-body strength that women cannot perform them. There are no women playing in the National Football League, Major League Baseball, the National Basketball Association, or the National Hockey League; and no

women boxing, or playing tennis against men in serious professional matches (except in mixed pairs). These leagues do not
exclude women. Women can try out for these teams if they want,
and if they beat out enough of the men, they will make the team.
But that has not happened yet. The strongest women simply are
not strong enough to compete with the strongest men in these
sports.

But major-league sports comprise only a tiny fraction of jobs.
There are plenty of other physical-labor jobs, and women can
perform almost all of them as well as men can. If you need to fill
a physical-labor job, you can approach it the way a professional
sports team would. Even if the team was historically all male, the
team no longer cares about gender (if it ever did). The team just
wants to *win!* The team wants the *best players*—regardless of gender. The team will not assume, just because an applicant is female,
that she is weaker than the male applicants. The team will conduct
strength and endurance tests if such tests are reasonably job-
related. Everyone, male and female, will take the tests. The
strongest applicants will get the jobs, be they male or female.

Of course, you are not *required* to conduct tests. But if a 150-
pound man and a 150-pound woman apply for a job, don't assume
that the man is stronger. Let them both test for the job. The test
does not have to be elaborate or lengthy. It can be short and simple. Don't have a height or weight requirement unless you have
substantial proof that a certain height or weight is *necessary* to perform the job. Some police and fire departments might still have
height or weight requirements, but that is government (public-
sector) employment. Sometimes the rules are a bit different in
public-sector employment than in private-sector employment.

No law requires that your workforce reflect the gender ratio
(roughly fifty-fifty) of the general population. As a matter of common sense, however, an all-male or nearly all-male workforce
does raise the suspicion that you discriminate against women. If

you have such a workforce and a male and a female with roughly equal qualifications apply for a job, you should probably hire the female. The more women you employ, especially in high places, the harder it is to accuse you of discriminating against women.

And be on the lookout for *men* claiming that they are being discriminated against by women in overwhelmingly female workplaces. If a man with good secretarial skills applies for a secretarial job at your company and all ten of your secretaries are female, and you reject the man for the job, don't be surprised if he sues for sex discrimination. He might even win.

Pregnancy, Adoption, and Maternity Leave

The law generally regards pregnancy discrimination as a form of sex discrimination. However, most states have their own employment laws pertaining to pregnancy, adoption, and maternity leave, so it is difficult to generalize about them in a short book such as this. You should look at the laws of your particular state.

Under federal law, employers with fifteen or more employees are required to treat pregnancy the same way they would treat any short-term illness.[28] Many *states'* laws go further: they require employers to allow pregnant women six, eight, or ten weeks off to give birth and recuperate (this is called "maternity leave") even if they would not ordinarily allow an employee that much time off for illness. (Unless the law or an employer's particular arrangement with its employees provides otherwise, the employer does not have to pay the woman during this period.) And if the employer has fifty or more employees, a pregnant employee might be entitled to up to twelve weeks off, under the federal Family and Medical Leave Act (FMLA). Pregnancy-related illnesses (such as morning sickness) ordinarily do not qualify as "disabilities" under the Americans with Disabilities Act, so the ADA provides little protection to pregnant women. Some pregnancy-related illnesses may qualify as "serious health conditions" entitling a pregnant woman to FMLA leave during the earlier stages (first six months) of pregnancy, but others will not.

Employers should not discriminate against pregnant women or women who might get pregnant. Not only is it illegal, it is counterproductive. Although pregnancy might occasionally divert a woman's time and attention away from her work, and giving birth will keep her out of the workplace for a few months, pregnancy and childbirth also give her an added incentive to do a good job for you. She now has another mouth to feed. She will need more money than a childless person does. She will be motivated to work harder to earn that extra money. She might seek a promotion or pay raise. The same is true of *men* whose wives get pregnant. They have more incentive, too.

Thus, discrimination against women due to their potential pregnancy is bad not only from a legal standpoint but also from a business standpoint. Many working mothers have very good child-care arrangements. According to *Working Mother* magazine, 83 percent of new mothers return to the labor force within six months after childbirth.[29] Many women want to earn as much money as their husbands earn. Equal earnings means equal power in the marital relationship. More and more men are content with having *less* power than their wives have. If their wives have successful careers, these men are willing to spend more time at home with the children. If the woman has a high-paying job, she and her husband might agree that *her* career will come first. Many male executives say, "I wish my wife had a high-paying job; then I could stay home more. I'd rather be home with my kids than working so hard." As Jane Bryant Quinn said in a column about married couples, "When she brings home more bacon, he makes more beds."[30]

One More Tip for Employers

If you fire a woman, consider hiring a woman to replace her, especially if you have a mostly male workforce. It will be much harder for the fired woman to claim sex discrimination. You don't *have to* replace her with a woman, but you should consider it, especially if you have few women employees in that job category.

One Other Exception to Treating Men and Women the Same

We mentioned that there are three exceptions to the rule that men and women should be treated the same: restrooms, manner of dress, and pregnancy. We also mentioned that occasionally there is a "bona fide occupational qualification" (BFOQ) that allows you to hire women only, or men only, for a particular job. For example, if you manufacture women's shoes and a man applies for a job modeling those shoes, you don't have to hire him. You can hire only women for that job if you want to.

There is another exception, a rather obvious one: office romance. If you wish to date a coworker, you can limit your choice to one gender or the other. But aside from that, the romance should be equal. "Traditional" gender roles, such as the male always (or nearly always) asking for the date and paying for the date, should be avoided. Women have declared they want to be treated equally with men. They want equal pay and equal job opportunity. They do not want to be dominated by men ("male domination"). Traditional gender roles in dating and courtship, such as the man making the decisions (asking for the date or deciding where to go on the date) and the man paying for the date, perpetuate male domination. They perpetuate the belief that men are supposed to be the aggressors, set the agenda, and control the finances. They lead men to "take control" over women.

Women should not allow this to occur. Women should seek the same equality when *dating* men as they do when *working with* men. Women should send a message that women do not want to be controlled by men. Over the past thirty years or so, women have made some effort to send that message. Women have rejected traditional gender roles in the workplace. Traditional gender roles in the workplace called for women to earn less money than men and to hold "softer," less prestigious jobs than men. Traditional gender roles called for women to become nurses while men became doctors, women to become legal secretaries while men became lawyers, and women to become senate aides while men became senators. Women have rejected these traditions and declared they want full equality with men in the workplace. Women have also demanded full equality with men outside the workplace in many aspects. Women want the same good tee times on the golf course that men have. Women don't want to pay more for clothes, haircuts, or insurance than men do.

But in some aspects of life, such as dating and courtship, many women continue to accept *in*equality with men. Inequality in dating and courtship, such as the woman always waiting for the man to call (for the first date, anyway) and always waiting for the man to pay (for the first date, anyway), perpetuates inequality in the workplace. If men are expected to take the lead in dating and courtship, men will expect to take the lead in the workplace, too.

If women will display the same assertiveness and financial self-determination in dating and courtship as men do (that is, women will ask men for dates and pay for dates as readily as men ask women for dates and pay for dates), women can end male domination in the workplace (and in life generally).

It follows that if two coworkers are going to date, it is best that they be of approximately equal rank within the company. If one dominates the other in the workplace—for example, if one is the boss of the other—it can lead to charges of sexual harassment.

This leads to our next chapter, "Ending Sexual Harassment."

Chapter Three
Ending Sexual Harassment

"Do not use liberty as an opportunity for the flesh." Galatians 5:13

Do Not Covet Thy Subordinate in a Sexual Way

Supervisors generally should not date or have sex with their subordinates, or even try to. If you are really attracted to your secretary or other subordinate, try to get him or her off your mind in that respect. Picture her or him less attractive. Do whatever it takes to avoid thinking of him or her in a sexual way. There is too great a chance that such a romantic relationship, even if occurs for awhile, will eventually end. When it ends, you will never be able to discipline or fire that subordinate without being accused of *sexual harassment* or *"retaliation."* It is illegal to fire an employee in retaliation for their complaining about sexual harassment. There is also the chance of blackmail—an employee showing an interest in you, hoping you will grab the bait so she or he can accuse you of sexual harassment.

If you find yourself becoming attracted to a subordinate, remember the words of Henry Kissinger when he was asked why a rather average-looking man like himself was able to date glamorous women such as actress Jill St. John: "Power is the ultimate aphrodisiac." What he meant was, if he were a nobody, glamorous women would have no interest in him. Only because he held a *position of power* were they interested.

What does this have to do with sexual harassment? Plenty. You have probably heard the cliché, "Sexual harassment isn't about sex, it's about power." Kissinger proved that that cliché is *half* true: Sexual harassment is about power.

But it is also about sex. In fact, it is usually more about sex than about power. When a male boss expresses a sexual interest in a female subordinate, the boss is not just showing off his power. (For the purpose of this explanation, we will use the example of a male boss and a female subordinate, but it could just as easily be the other way around.) He is thinking about *sex*, not power. His power, however, might make certain things happen. It might make him a bit more confident that the subordinate will accept his invitation for a date. It might also make the subordinate more interested in the boss, not because she fears the consequences of turning him down, but because she *genuinely* finds him more attractive than she would if he had no "power."

Women will sometimes flirt with or be interested in a man who is their boss yet would not be interested in him if he were of equal rank to them. They are attracted to his "power" more than they are attracted to him, really. Not that they are looking for anything in return. They are not necessarily looking for a raise or promotion or job security. They are simply intrigued by the thought of dating a man with a little "power," just as men are intrigued by dating women with power.

This dynamic is indeed gender-neutral. Men are sexually attracted to powerful women just as women are sexually attracted to powerful men. Power is, as Kissinger said, the ultimate aphrodisiac *regardless of which gender holds the power.* Men are often attracted to women executives and women politicians who would not be so attractive to these men if these women were waitresses and sales clerks. These men are also attracted to waitresses and sales clerks, but a waitress or sales clerk might have to be more physically attractive than a woman executive or politician to arouse sexual interest in these men. Some women probably think that women with power are a turn*off* to men. Maybe *some* men are turned off by them, but many men are attracted to them, just as many women are attracted to men with power.

So if you are a male boss and you think the attraction between you and a female subordinate is mutual, ask yourself this question: If you were not her boss, would she be attracted to you? If your answer is no, do not attempt to romance her. She is intrigued by your power, and is possibly, though not necessarily, trying to get ahead in your company. A male subordinate might try to do the same with a female boss. There is usually no legal problem if that subordinate does get ahead in your company. But if that subordinate does not, that subordinate will blame *you* and might sue you and your company. Do not succumb to temptation without thinking through all the ramifications.

If you are quite certain that the subordinate is genuinely interested in you and would be even if you were not his or her boss, then nonetheless tread very carefully. It is legally unwise to date a subordinate, but if you really want to, try to make sure that the attraction is mutual and has nothing to do with the power you have over her. If she has given you no hint whatsoever that she is interested in you, don't ask her out.

If you do ask out a subordinate and she says no, or she gives you some lame excuse ("Uh, I have company coming in this weekend"), don't ask again. Forget about it. If it doesn't happen easily, give up. Don't be persistent in trying to get a date with a subordinate. You are asking for trouble. If she or he turns you down or gives you an excuse, don't pout or walk off in a huff. Any anger or frustration you exhibit will be noticed and can be used against you by that subordinate if you ever have to fire, demote, or take some other type of adverse employment action against her. She will say it is because she turned you down for a date.

What about dating coworkers, that is, people of the same rank or somewhat higher rank than you? There is no problem with that. Just remember, though, the higher up you are in the company, the fewer the employees you can safely attempt to romance.

Should your company adopt a no-dating rule: No employee can date a coemployee? Or a rule requiring the two employees (or just the subordinate employee) to sign a form indicating that the relationship is totally consensual? There is rarely if ever a good reason for such rules. If any employee complains to you that she is being bothered by or pursued too aggressively by a coworker and asks you to intercede and tell the pursuer to stop, do so. Whenever you receive a complaint that someone is being sexually harassed, ask the victim *what she wants you to do about it*. If she is unsure, tell her there is little or nothing you can do about it— other than reminding all your employees of your sexual harassment policy—until she decides what she wants you to do about it. Don't be afraid to tell her to first try to work the problem out herself with the harasser. The harasser will usually be angrier if the victim goes *over his head* or *behind his back* (that is, complains to the harasser's boss or to other people in the company) than if the victim complains to the harasser directly. Nearly all men will stop harassing a woman once the woman makes *absolutely clear* to him that she is not interested in him. The problem is when the woman gives *mixed signals* or has already had a lengthy, intimate relationship with the man. Quite often a woman will call a lawyer and complain that a male boss or coworker has been harassing her for a long time. She usually wants to know if she has a good sexual harassment case.

"Did you ever accept one of his invitations?" the lawyer will ask.

"Yeah, a few times," the woman will reply.

"When was the last time?" the lawyer will ask.

"Last week," she will reply.

"If he's so bad, why did you accept?"

"I didn't know he was that bad. Actually, we went out a number of times. But I don't want to go out with him anymore. I want him to leave me alone. He has a problem with that."

"Did you feel in any way coerced to go out with him?"

"Not really."

These cases are like those domestic violence cases in which the man pushes the woman around for the twelfth time, she forgives him for the twelfth time, and then the thirteenth time he *really* gets violent. If she had dumped him the first or second time, he'd be long gone and have forgotten about her. But after twelve times, these men become like dogs who keep finding food that a sympathetic person left for them. That person will have great difficulty getting rid of the dog now. The dog is so accustomed to the food that the dog will growl, bite, and bark ever louder now. The dog thinks he has a "right" to that person's food. The dog thinks he "owns" that person.

Be patient, however. If the harassment victim needs your assistance to formulate a plan to deal with the problem (such as when she is being harassed by a supervisor), assist her. Many states have laws prescribing what an employer should do when an employee complains of sexual harassment. Check your state's laws for guidance on this.

Should your company adopt a policy prohibiting supervisors and executives from dating subordinates? That is a close call. Such a policy reduces the risk of sexual harassment lawsuits but might not be good human resource management. The opportunity for romance is an important—though unofficial—employee "benefit." A company where unmarried men and women have opportunities to find romance will attract more and better job applicants and have better employee morale than a company that prohibits such opportunities.

We emphasize the word *unmarried*, however. *Extra*marital romance is a morale *buster*, not booster. A married boss dating an unmarried (or married) subordinate, or an unmarried boss dating a married subordinate will offend most employees who witness it or know about it. It will also offend most *jurors*. Juries are more likely to "award" a sexual harassment victim big damages if the harasser was married than if he was unmarried. In a jury's view, an unmarried supervisor is free to at least *try* to get a date or establish a romantic relationship with a subordinate— not to be *too* persistent about it, but to at least ask once. A married man or woman is not free in this regard.

Sexually Hostile Work Environment

There are two types of sexual harassment, but it is not always easy to distinguish one from the other. Nor is there much reason to. You can be sued for either. The two types are *quid pro quo* and *sexually hostile work environment. Quid pro quo* sexual harassment occurs when a boss makes employment decisions based on whether a subordinate will have sexual or romantic relations with him. It need not be explicit (such as, "Go to bed with me or you're fired"). If a boss asks a secretary for a date and she turns him down, and a year later he fires her for being late for the fifteenth time (after giving her stern warnings the twelfth, thirteenth, and fourteenth times), don't be surprised if she sues him and the company for quid pro quo sexual harassment. She will claim that the *real* reason he fired her was that she refused to go out with him a year earlier.

Sexually hostile work environment refers to sexual advances, sexual conduct, or sexual comments that are so severe or so repetitious that they make it more difficult for the victim to do her job.[31] They must be that offensive in order to be legally classified as "sexual harassment," at least under federal law and the laws of virtually every state. And they must be "unwelcome." If the boss was not aware of the employee's displeasure with the conduct or comments, and the employee did nothing to make him aware (she didn't tell him and she didn't tell any other person of authority), and the conduct, comments, or advances were not that bad, she will probably lose.

Frequently people ask whether one sort of conduct or another comprises sexual harassment. "If I look at my secretary's legs, is that sexual harassment?" "My boss told me a dirty joke; is that sexual harassment?" "Our top customer—a real playboy— keeps asking our saleswoman for a date, and he always hugs her and puts his arm around her; can she claim harassment?" (This is called "third-party sexual harassment.") "Our sales clerk objects to our selling *Penthouse* on the magazine rack; she claims it is sexual harassment." "Is it okay for one of our guys to have the *Sports Illustrated* swimsuit calendar over his desk, or another one of our guys to have a picture of his girlfriend in a string bikini?" "If we give a raise to secretary A, who is sleeping with her boss, but we don't give a raise to secretary B, who is not sleeping with her boss, can secretary B sue us for sexual harassment or sex discrimination?" (This is called "sexual favoritism.")

The answer is usually no. If that is all that happened—one little incident or a few little incidents—that is not sexual harassment. To be sexual harassment, the conditions have to be severe or repetitious. Grabbing a female employee's breast is severe. If it happens once, she might have a case. But the less severe the conduct, the more repetitious it has to be to amount to sexual harassment. If the conduct was not repetitious or severe, but the subordinate nonetheless complained about it and asked you to put a stop to it, and you did not put a stop to it, that might or might not be sexual harassment. It would depend on the circumstances.

Sexual objects, sexual jokes, sexual E-mail, sexual humor via Internet, sexy calendars, very sexy photographs of boyfriends, girlfriends, or strangers, and very sexual innuendoes might, if severe or repetitious enough, comprise sexual harassment.

Also, it is usually a good idea not to allow employees to wear clothing that is too revealing. Such clothing invites jokes and harassment.

However, there is something you should know. Most people who sue for sexual harassment are *terminated* employees. Especially in private-sector, nonunion workplaces, it is quite rare for an employee who is still employed by a company to sue that company for sexual harassment. Most employees who sue for sexual harassment are employees who were fired or laid off. They are angry about getting fired or laid off, so they dredge up sexual comments and sexual incidents they heard while employed in their former job situations. They claim they objected to those comments and incidents and that their objections led to their being terminated.

Then there are employees who were not fired or laid off but claim that the harassment was so severe that they could not stand it any longer, so they quit (this is called "constructive discharge"). Then there are employees who sense that they are *about to* get fired or laid off, so they sue for sexual harassment hoping the employer will fear firing them or laying them off.

But rarely, at least in private-sector, nonunion workplaces, does an employee who is still working there and who is not on the verge of getting fired or laid off sue for sexual harassment.

In fact, that is true of discrimination cases in general. Probably 80 percent (or even more) are brought by employees who were fired or laid off. The percentage is less in government employment and unionized workplaces. That is, government employees and unionized employees *are more likely to sue while still employed* than private-sector, nonunion employees are. That is because government employees and unionized employees usually feel they can sue and not get fired. They feel almost immune from getting fired. They also have many layers of grievance procedures available to them without having to pay a lawyer.

Who Harasses? Who Accuses?

Do not try to "profile" sexual harassers or sexual harass*ees*. They come in all shapes, sizes, colors, and ages.

However, there are two categories of men who are more likely than other men to be *accused of* (but not necessarily guilty of) sexual harassment: (1) men with foreign accents (especially men of color with foreign accents) and (2) male executives whose fathers or mothers own or founded the company. Why? As for men with foreign accents, particularly Africans, Latinos, Middle Easterners, and Asians, it is conceivable that they are more likely to behave in a way that American women perceive as "harassment," but it is also conceivable that American women (white women, anyway) perceive these men to be easy targets. Women think a jury will more likely believe a white American woman than a dark man who speaks with a heavy African, Iranian, Israeli, or Indian accent.

As for sons of company founders, some of them are rich spoiled brats who really do harass women subordinates, while others are merely perceived by women to be such.

In any event, dark men with foreign accents and white men whose fathers founded the business should be *very* careful about approaching subordinates for romance, or even mentioning sexual topics to subordinates.

As for women who accuse, a significant percentage of women who sue for sexual harassment have also claimed at various times in their lives that they were battered or sexually abused by men. Frequently a woman who has been divorced once or twice and has held numerous low-level jobs with numerous different employers accuses a company executive, who has been married forty years, of sexually harassing her. He denies it. It is difficult to know who is telling the truth. The man has had a much more stable life and career, which tends to make him more credible. On the other hand, there are men with stable lives and careers who prey upon vulnerable women.

And to repeat what was said a few paragraphs ago: private-sector, nonunion employees (as opposed to government employees and union employees) usually don't sue for sexual harassment unless they have been fired or otherwise terminated. So if a secretary complains that someone is looking at her legs or telling dirty jokes, you can and should take appropriate action to put a stop to it, but you should not be excessively worried that she will sue. She probably will not sue unless you terminate her (although it is difficult to generalize about this; the probability will depend on numerous factors).

Miscellaneous Types of Sexual Harassment

As mentioned before, there are some other types of sexual harassment: *third-party sexual harassment* and *sexual favoritism.*

Third-party sexual harassment occurs when an employee complains that someone associated with the company but not an employee of the company is sexually harassing the employee. For example, a waitress will complain that a drunk customer is sexually harassing her. Employers who serve a lot of alcohol are probably more likely to be sued for "third-party" sexual harassment than those who do not.

There have been few third-party sexual harassment suits. That is because few victims of third-party sexual harassment get fired for complaining about it. A customer cannot fire your employee. As was said a few paragraphs ago, employees who sue for sexual harassment are usually *terminated* employees.

Sexual favoritism occurs when employee A is given a raise or promotion, or is retained rather than terminated in a company downsizing, because s/he is having some kind of sexual or romantic relationship with the boss. Employee B, who has the same job title and boss but is *not* given a raise or promotion, or *is* terminated in the downsizing, sues for sex discrimination. Employee B claims that employee B was discriminated against "because of sex." The law is not too clear on whether employee B has a case, but if employee B can prove that employee B was at least as good as, or better than, employee A, then employee B may well have a case. Sexual favoritism is a form of sexual harassment or sex discrimination.

Use your common sense and do not engage in or tolerate such types of harassment/discrimination. If you must tell your biggest customer to stop harassing your saleswoman, do so (as gently and diplomatically as possible, of course).

Finally, be aware that sexual harassment is illegal even if the harasser is harassing someone of his or her own gender.[32] It is illegal for a man to sexually harass a man, and it is illegal for a woman to sexually harass a woman.

Chapter Four
Ending Other Kinds of Discrimination

"Do unto each employee as you would if that employee's gender, race, religion, national origin, and age were exactly what you wanted them to be." (the "golden rule" of employment law)

Follow the "Golden Rule" of Employment Law

The "golden rule" of employment law is stated above: Do unto each employee as you would if that employee's gender, race, religion, national origin, and age were exactly what you wanted them to be. This may sound like a recapitulation of the book's earlier chapters, but it is more. It is another simple mental exercise to help you avoid discriminating.

If you are a white manager and are contemplating firing a black employee, ask yourself: "If this black employee were white and performing the job exactly as he is performing it and saying the same things and exhibiting the same attitudes and behaviors as he is in fact saying and exhibiting, would I be firing this employee?" Think hard. If your answer is yes (that is, you would fire him anyway), then you probably can fire him. If your answer is no, then don't fire him. If your answer is no, it means race is influencing your decision.

If you are a woman contemplating firing a man, use the same type of thought process: "If this employee were a woman rather than a man, would I be firing this employee?" If your answer is yes (that is, you would fire this employee anyway), then you probably can fire him. If your answer is no, then don't fire him. If your answer is no, it means gender is influencing your decision.

If you are fifty-five years old and are contemplating firing a fifty-year-old employee, ask yourself: "Would I be firing this employee if he were thirty-five years old?" The reason you should use thirty-five years of age rather than your own age is that some people think that people their own age (and even a few years younger) are "too old" for a particular job. There are fifty-five-year-old executives who think a fifty-year-old is "too old" for some jobs.

The analysis gets a bit trickier if more than one of these traits differs from yours, but you can figure it out. If you are a fifty-five-year-old white male contemplating firing a fifty-year-old black female, ask yourself: "If this employee were a thirty-five-year-old white male performing the job exactly as this employee is in fact performing it, and saying the same things and exhibiting the same attitudes and behaviors that this employee is in fact saying and exhibiting, would I be firing this employee?" If your honest answer is yes, then you probably can fire her.

If you suspect that the employee's being of a different *religion* or *national origin* influences you, ask yourself: "Would I be firing this employee if he were the same religion and national origin as me?" If your honest answer is yes, then you probably can fire him.

Religion Discrimination

Employers cannot discriminate against employees due to religion. Furthermore, employers are required to "reasonably accommodate" their employees' religious practices. If a Muslim woman wants to cover up her body so that only her face, hands, and feet are showing—as required by her religion—you probably have to allow her to do so even if it conflicts with your dress code or uniform. If a Jewish employee needs to leave work at 5:00 P.M. on Friday to attend religious services or to take Saturday off completely, you probably have to allow this. Whether you *must* allow him to do so depends on how much of a hardship it would be to you if he left at 5:00 P.M. Friday or took Saturday off.

You may have the right to inquire whether an employee who seeks a religious accommodation is really a follower of that religion, however. Some employees suddenly claim to follow a religion just so they can take a few days off or work reduced hours. They pretend to observe that religion's holy days. If you have reason to believe that someone is faking his religion or exaggerating some religious requirement, you can require him to provide documentation that he really is a follower of that religion and that the religion really does have that requirement. But be careful. If you require Jews and Muslims to prove they are Jewish or Muslim but don't require Christians to prove they are Christian, that might be illegal discrimination.

What about *your* religious rights as a business owner or manager? Do you have the right to put up Christmas decorations? What if a non-Christian complains about them? Would you have to take the decorations down? Can you *forbid* Christmas decorations? Can you offer Bible-study sessions? Can you *require* people to attend them? Can you put up the Ten Commandments? Can you require employees to attend church? Can you invite employees to attend church with you?

It is difficult to answer these questions in this book because the answers might depend on which state you are in. Different states have different legal standards pertaining to religion in the workplace. Furthermore, the answer will be very different if you are a government employer than if you are a private-sector employer. The "separation of church and state" applies to government employers but generally does not apply to private-sector employers. Therefore, private-sector employers have more religious freedom than government employers do.

Some general words of caution are in order, however. First, there is a difference between religious *decorations* and religious *services.* There are few if any cases in which a private-sector employer has been sued (and lost) for putting up religious decorations. If an employee were to complain, you might have to take down the decorations that are in that employee's immediate work area. If employees of other religions wish to put up their own religious decorations at their own workstations, you probably have to let them.

As for religious *services* (prayer services), you probably have the right to *offer* them but not the right to *compel* employees to attend. You cannot punish or discriminate against employees who do not attend. And keep this in mind: Employers who conduct or offer prayer services in the workplace are virtually inviting employee lawsuits even if the employees have little chance of winning these suits. If an employee is fired, not promoted, or not hired, he or she will likely claim to be a victim of religious discrimination. He or she will claim that the employer prefers to hire, promote, and retain people of a certain religion. Employers who conduct or offer religious activities in the workplace probably do prefer employees who are of the employer's religion. While it is legal to express your religious views, it is illegal to discriminate against employees because their religious views differ from yours. So be careful. Be especially careful if the religion your company or organization espouses is not a mainstream religion. A jury might be less likely to sympathize with your company or organization.

If your company or organization serves a particular religious purpose (for example, if it is a church, synagogue, or mosque), the rules are somewhat different. Only members of your religion may be qualified to hold certain jobs. Religion may be a *bona fide occupational qualification* for certain jobs. But other jobs can be held by members of any religion, and you do not have the right to discriminate on the basis of religion when hiring, promoting, and retaining people for these other jobs.

Disability Discrimination

The golden rule of employment law is sometimes helpful when analyzing situations involving *disabled* employees, but not always.

If the person's disability does not affect his or her job performance, or affects it in a minor way, ask yourself: "Would I be firing this disabled employee if he or she were *not* disabled?" If your answer is yes—you would be firing the employee even if he or she were not disabled—you can fire the employee and probably not be held liable for disability discrimination (and hopefully not even get sued).

However, some disabilities do affect job performance. Some disabilities make it very difficult or impossible to perform certain jobs. That is why they are called *dis*abilities. Therefore, the analysis in a disability discrimination case is often more complicated than it is in a race, age, sex, or religion discrimination case. The laws prohibiting race, age, sex, and religion discrimination are based on the assumption that race, sex, age, and religion have *no* effect on job performance. The laws prohibiting disability discrimination, on the other hand, are based on the assumption that many disabilities *do* affect job performance. In fact, some disabilities make job performance *very difficult* or *impossible*. If the disability makes the person unable to do the job, you generally do not have to hire or retain that person.

However, disability discrimination law also assumes that (1) *not all* disabilities affect job performance, (2) a particular disability might affect the job performance of *some* employees who have that disability but not *other* employees who have that disability, and (3) even if a disability does make it difficult or impossible for an employee to do the job, there may exist some type of inexpensive mechanism or accommodation that enables that employee to do the job as well as the employer's nondisabled employees do.

Consequently, if there exists such a mechanism or accommodation, the employer is required to provide it. If there does not exist such a mechanism or accommodation and the disabled employee simply cannot perform the job as well as the employer's nondisabled employees do, the employer need not hire or retain that disabled employee.

In other words, disability discrimination law protects people who *can do the job*. Those who can*not* do the job even with whatever mechanisms or accommodations are reasonably available are *not* protected by the disability discrimination laws. You do not have to hire or retain them.

Thus, employers should not have a *stereotypical view* of disabilities. For example, an employer should not *assume*, just because an employee suffers from depression (which is usually a "disability" under the Americans with Disabilities Act, or ADA), that the employee's job performance will be less than that of employees who do not suffer from depression. It might or might not be less. Employers should look at each disabled employee as an individual.

Here are the general principles of disability discrimination law: If an employee's disability prevents the employee from performing the essential functions of the job in accordance with your company's standards (that is, prevents him from performing them as well as your nondisabled employees perform them), you can terminate him; however, you first must consider whether there exists some mechanism or accommodation that might enable him to perform up to those standards. If such a mechanism or accommodation exists and you can provide it without undue hardship (financial or other type of hardship) to your company, you must provide it.

You can require the employee to pay that part of the cost of the accommodation that is an undue hardship to your company.[33] However, you must first try to determine whether tax credits or deductions might offset the cost of the accommodation, and also explore whether funding might be available from an outside source, such as a state rehabilitation agency.

These requirements are called *reasonable accommodation*. If no reasonably affordable mechanism or accommodation exists that will enable the employee to perform up to your company's standards, then you need not hire or retain that employee. For example, if your company requires all its clerical people to be able to type at least seventy words per minute accurately, and a disabled employee or job applicant cannot type more than fifty words per minute accurately even with whatever accommodations or mechanisms could reasonably be provided to him or her, you need not hire or retain that employee/job applicant.

The important point to remember is that you do not have to tolerate lesser productivity from a disabled employee than you do from an employee with no disability. You can if you want, but you don't have to. Disabled employees can be held to the same standards as nondisabled workers. However, you do have to explore whether a lesser-performing disabled employee might be able to perform as well as your nondisabled employees if he or she is provided with some type of reasonably inexpensive mechanism or accommodation.

Also, you have to be careful in the job-interviewing process not to ask employees if they have disabilities or to question them about disabilities. You can ask them if they can perform the various aspects of the job and to demonstrate that they can. Asking them to submit to a medical examination or to provide medical documentation is sometimes permitted in the hiring process.

Asking current employees (as opposed to job applicants) to submit to a medical examination is also permitted if job related and consistent with business necessity.[34]

What types of accommodations might you have to provide a disabled employee to enable him or her to perform the essential functions of a particular job in accordance with company standards? There are manuals on this topic and thus no need to list them all here. Most are a matter of common sense. One accommodation you may have to provide is sick time and light duty. You may have to provide extra sick days, light duty, a leave of absence, or some scheduling flexibility to an employee to accommodate his or her disability. At some point, however, if the employee is absent too much, the employee will no longer be considered a "qualified individual" under the disability discrimination laws. In essence, he will no longer be regarded as "qualified" for the job, and thus can be legally terminated.

Disability discrimination law can be rather tricky and difficult to explain in a short book and, like all types of discrimination, the answers to specific questions often depend on which state you are in. Generally speaking, though, common sense and decency will suffice to keep employers out of trouble and cost them nothing. Employers can easily comply with the disability discrimination laws without giving up anything in productivity or discipline.

The legal definition of disability under the Americans with Disabilities Act ("ADA") is rather vague: "...a physical or mental impairment that substantially limits one or more of the major life activities of [the employee]."[35] An employee also has a "disability" under the ADA if he has a "record of such an impairment" or is "regarded as having such an impairment."[36] For example, an employee who was committed to a mental hospital ten years ago might be "regarded" by some people as still mentally impaired today even if he has a "clean bill of health." He also has a "record of such an impairment." Short-term illnesses and short-term injuries are not disabilities. The ADA does not list all the conditions that are and are not disabilities. To some extent, employers (and employees) must use their common sense in deciding whether the employee has a "disability."

Many employers were worried that the ADA had defined the word *disability* so broadly that every problem every employee had would be considered a "disability" and the employer would have to put up with it. But that has not happened. Even though courts often accept the employee's claim of being "disabled," courts rarely require employers to put up with substandard or erratic performance by a disabled employee. As long as the employer makes some reasonable effort to help the employee perform up to standards, the employer is rarely held liable even if the effort is unsuccessful (that is, if the employee is unable to perform up to standards with the employer's effort). Most employees who have brought ADA cases have lost (or have settled very cheaply rather than lose entirely).[37] Just being "disabled" doesn't get an employee very far in a disability discrimination lawsuit. Furthermore, in 1999 and again in 2002 the U.S. Supreme Court held that the definition of *disability* is not as broad as many had thought.[38]

Most courts have taken a particularly dim view of employees who claim "disabilities" that are not really disabilities or who claim to have conditions that are disabilities but do not really have these conditions (they falsely claim to have these conditions). If an employee claims to have a condition that is a disability and asks that you "accommodate" it and you are not sure whether the employee really does have that condition, ordinarily you have the right to ask the employee to furnish medical proof that he has this condition. This is particularly true of nonobvious ("invisible") disabilities such as mental disabilities, headaches, depression, learning disabilities, certain types of back pain, and other disabilities that an employee can fake or exaggerate. Just because an employee claims he has one of these conditions does not mean the employer has to take the employee's word for it. The employer can ask the employee to produce his medical records to show he has this condition. If the employee refuses to produce the records or if the records do not indicate that he has this condition, the employee must somehow prove to the employer that he has the condition. If he doesn't, the employer need not provide the accommodation.[39] Disability, like religion, is often invisible. That means it can be faked or exaggerated. Employers have a right to ascertain whether the employee is faking or exaggerating it.

Age Discrimination

Many people misunderstand age discrimination law. They think age discrimination law makes it illegal to terminate older workers. Or they think employers have to allow older workers to slow down and be less productive than younger workers.

They are mistaken. Older workers can be terminated just as younger workers can. If an older worker is unable to perform the job as well as most of your younger workers, you can terminate him. This is true even if his inability is due to the effects of aging. You are thereby terminating him not because of age, but because of job performance.

If, on the other hand, he *is* able to perform the job as well as many of your younger workers, you must treat him no differently than you treat them.

That is not only what *the law* says; it is what *the Bible* says. "Honor the elders. Let the elders who rule well be counted worthy of double honor" (1 Tim 5:17). "Likewise you younger people, submit yourselves to your elders" (1 Pet 5:5). So if an elderly employee is "ruling well," or performing well, don't fire her just because she is elderly. But if she is not performing well, you need not "honor" her with continued employment.

Basically, the law requires you to make an assumption: that age (if forty or older) has no effect on job performance.[40] But obviously that assumption is not always correct. Some workers, especially in highly physical occupations, become less effective at their jobs as they get older. For example, there are no (none we can think of, anyway; perhaps we are overlooking someone) major-league baseball, football, basketball, hockey, or tennis players over the age of forty-five. Only a handful are over forty. Hundreds of major-league athletes in their early forties are "cut from the team" (terminated) each year. They can no longer perform their jobs as well as younger athletes can. Their diminished ability is due to the effects of aging and the general wear and tear that eventually takes a toll on a major-league athlete.

If they are cut from the team due to their diminished ability, does that mean they are victims of "age discrimination?" No. They were terminated, not because of age, but because of job performance. True, their job performance declined due to age. But they were terminated due to job performance, not age. If a twenty-two-year-old were performing no better than these forty-two-year-olds, he would be terminated, too.

From his late teens until his early forties, baseball pitcher Nolan Ryan could throw a baseball a blazing ninety-eight miles per hour. But as he approached age forty-five, he no longer could. He could no longer throw even ninety-three miles per hour. Younger pitchers on the team, or who were applying for pitching jobs on the team, could throw ninety-three miles per hour or more. So the team had a right to terminate Ryan and replace him with a pitcher who could throw ninety-three miles per hour. That is not age discrimination. (Actually, the team did not "terminate" Ryan. Like many athletes who know their abilities have diminished and that the team has a right to replace them with someone with more ability, Ryan retired.)

Suppose, however, that Ryan could still throw ninety-three miles per hour when he was forty-five years old, or fifty years old. If the team terminated him at age fifty because the team simply *assumed* he would no longer be able to throw ninety-three miles per hour, *that would have been age discrimination.*

That is what we mean when we say age discrimination law is about *assumptions*. Remember what we said about gender discrimination: don't *assume*, just because a 150-pound person is female, that she cannot perform a job as well as a 150-pound man. Maybe she can, maybe she can't. Don't make assumptions just because she is female and he is male. Get the facts. It may well be that that particular woman cannot perform the job as well as that particular man. But don't just *assume* it because she is female.

So too with age discrimination. Don't *assume*, just because an employee is older, that he is unable to perform as well as younger employees perform. Don't assume that older workers ("older" being defined as forty or older) are physically or mentally slower, more apt to retire, or more apt to get sick or die soon, than younger workers are. Some are, some aren't.

However, if for whatever reason (including age) an employee cannot perform as well as your younger employees perform, you need not retain that employee. As with handicap discrimination law, if age has caused the employee to be less effective than your other employees, you can terminate that employee. You can terminate an employee for being less effective than your other employees, but not simply because of his age. So focus on *job performance* and *ignore age*. That is easy in baseball because baseball performance is easily measured in numbers. The speed of Nolan Ryan's fastball was easily measured by a machine. His overall job performance was easily measured by familiar (to baseball fans) statistics such as his "earned run average," strikeouts, and win-loss record. But in most other types of jobs, performance is not so easily measured. When performance is difficult to measure, managers are more apt to consider age.

Managers should not do that. Managers should ignore age. How do you *ignore* age? Easy. When contemplating terminating an older worker, pretend the worker has a full head of hair (and the same *color* hair the employee had when young), unwrinkled skin, and all other outward appearances of youth. Pretend you have no idea how old the worker is. Then ask yourself: "Is this not-too-effective worker performing as well as my younger workers?" If he or she is not—in other words, if his or her job performance is worse than that of *all* your younger workers in the same job category and perhaps some similar job categories—you can terminate this older employee. But if even *one* younger worker is a worse performer than the older (forty or older) worker, *reconsider* whom to terminate. Perhaps you should terminate the *younger* one, or maybe *both* of them.

Make sure you have some older workers on your workforce, even if it means you occasionally have to discriminate in favor of an older worker or older job applicant and against a younger one. Although it is illegal to discriminate against someone on the basis of their being *over* forty (actually, forty or over), it is legal to discriminate against someone on the basis of their being *under* forty (except in two states, which prohibit *all* forms of age discrimination so long as the employee is over eighteen). Therefore, except in those two states, discrimination *in favor of* older workers is generally legal. Having a workplace that reflects the age of the general population (or is *above* the age of the general population) reduces your likelihood of being accused of age discrimination.

Tips to Avoid Becoming a Victim of Age Discrimination

What can older workers do to prevent being discriminated against? Three things: exercise, education, and mentoring. Exercise enables older workers to stay in good physical shape and avoid getting overweight. Physically fit older workers are far less likely to be discriminated against than physically unfit ones. You don't have to dye your hair or tattoo your body. You can "look your age." But try to look as good for your age as you possibly can. Make it your *skills* that stand out—not your age.[41]

Older workers should consider taking college courses and other "continuing education" courses. This demonstrates their willingness and ability to learn and change. It is sad to read about older workers being downsized out of jobs they have held for many years. But whose fault is it? Is it the fault of the employer, or is it the fault of the employee? Some employees get complacent as they get older, do not maintain their skills and good attitude, and do not learn new skills. When they get fired, they think it is because of their age. Sometimes they are right. But more often it is because they got *complacent, did not maintain their skills and good attitude*, and *did not learn new skills*. In those situations, the firing is not age discrimination. Such employees would have been fired even if they were twenty-five years old.

Older workers should mentor younger workers and help them climb the corporate ladder. If you help a younger worker and she later becomes a CEO, and you need a job someday, maybe she will return the favor and hire you.

Another problem with older employees is that they become too dependent on *one* employer—*their* employer. If that employer terminates them, they are devastated. They fear they will not be able to find a job elsewhere at their age. But again, whose fault is that? The employer's? Or their own? Employees should maintain *employability*, so that if an employer fires them or lays them off, they can go out and find another job without too much difficulty. Employers should encourage this. Employers should encourage employees to maintain their skills, learn new skills, and learn new technology. Getting dumped by an employer is like getting dumped by a girlfriend or boyfriend: painful though it is, the pain goes away as soon as the dumped one finds another girlfriend or boyfriend. An employee who quickly finds another job is considerably less likely to sue you than one who suffers a long period of unemployment.

Note that we use a *boyfriend-girlfriend* analogy, not a *marriage* analogy. Some employees are as devastated by losing a job as they would be if their spouse died or divorced them. They have no right to feel this way. They were not "married" to the employer. They had no lifetime contract with the employer, as husbands and wives have with each other. They probably had no contract at all. They were, in most cases, employees-at-will, meaning, according to the laws of most states, that they had the right to *quit* at any time without explanation, and the employer had the right to *terminate* them at any time without explanation (so long as the employer was not motivated by the employee's race, color, national origin, gender, or other illegal reason). They should simply move on and find a new employer. Employers should help them prepare for this eventuality by encouraging them to keep themselves in good vocational shape so they are attractive to other employers.

Here is a "parable" that illustrates the point.

The Parable of the Boyfriends and the Girlfriends

Two men had attractive girlfriends ("girlfriend" and "boyfriend" are acceptable words to refer to romantic companions even if the "girl" and "boy" are both well over eighteen; this is an exception to the "rule" that says men should not refer to women over eighteen as "girls"). The first man got complacent about the relationship and put on fifty pounds of flab. When his girlfriend dumped him without explanation, he felt hurt. But the hurt intensified when he found that he was unable, due to being so out of shape, to land another attractive woman. So he kept trying to win back the girlfriend, which made him (and her) even more miserable. He became a nuisance to her.

The second man also got dumped without explanation, but he had stayed strong and fit, so he easily found another attractive woman to date and quickly forgot about the woman who dumped him. In fact, the woman who dumped him eventually got jealous and tried to win him back, without success.

The moral of the story is, an employee who stays "in shape" is less likely to bother (sue) an employer if the employer "dumps" (fires) him. He'll find another job easily. This is true even if he is an older employee. Although some employers discriminate against older employees, many do not. Many *prefer* older employees.

So encourage your employees to stay in good vocational "shape." If you eventually fire them or lay them off, they will find new jobs quickly and be less likely to try to drag you down with them. Furthermore, you might just decide *not* to fire them or lay them off. An "in shape" employee is one you won't want to lose!

Sexual Orientation Discrimination

If you are a business owner or manager in one of the thirteen states (plus the District of Columbia) that prohibit discrimination based on sexual orientation, you should follow the "golden rule of employment law" when you are dealing with gay, lesbian, and bisexual employees—to the extent you know who they are. If you know or suspect that an employee (or job applicant) is gay, lesbian, or bisexual, and you are contemplating firing, demoting, denying a promotion to, or not hiring this employee/applicant, ask yourself: What if this employee/applicant were heterosexual? Would you be taking such action? If your answer is yes, then you can probably fire, demote, not promote, or not hire this employee/applicant and not be held liable in a sexual orientation discrimination case. But if your answer is no, then don't take such action.

It is better, of course, that you *not* know who they are and *not speculate about* who they are. If you do not know or speculate about who they are, it will be difficult for them to accuse you of discriminating against them.

Therefore, *ignore* your employees' homosexuality or bisexuality. Don't ask about it. Don't tell about it. Don't think about it. The less you know about it, the better.

Some of you might feel that laws protecting homosexuals from discrimination conflict with the Bible. The Bible forbids homosexuality (Lev 18:22; 20:13; 1 Cor 6:9), but there is no conflict. These laws do not require you to *approve of* homosexuality. They require you *not to discriminate against* employees for being homosexual. In other words, these laws permit you to disapprove, in your heart and mind, of homosexuality, but do not permit you to play God. The law is the same as stated in the *Catechism of the Catholic Church*, which requires acceptance of homosexuals but not of homosexuality. "They must be accepted with respect, compassion, and sensitivity. Every sign of unjust discrimination in their regard should be avoided" (*Catechism*, par. 2358). The Presbyterian General Assembly has called for the passage of laws forbidding discrimination based on sexual orientation in employment.[42]

If you disapprove of homosexuality, don't express your disapproval to your employees. If you express it and then you fire one of them, he or she will accuse you of discrimination. *Ignore* your employees' homosexuality (if any).[43]

There have been very few sexual orientation discrimination cases. One reason is obvious: To bring such a suit, the employee ordinarily has to "come out." The employee has to declare in his or her court complaint—which in most states is a document available for public inspection—that he or she is homosexual or bisexual. Many homosexual and bisexual employees do not want to do that.

Some employees who sue for sexual orientation discrimination, however, are not homosexual or bisexual. They are, or at least they claim to be, heterosexual. What are they suing for, then? This may sound hard to believe, but they are suing based on what is called "perceived" homosexuality. The boss called them a "fag" or otherwise "identified" them as gay or lesbian. In some states (such as Massachusetts), if an employee is fired or otherwise treated badly because the employer believed or "identified" him as gay or bisexual, the employee can sue for sexual orientation discrimination. But these employees must make potentially embarrassing declarations in their lawsuits: that their employer "perceived" them to be gay or bisexual.

In any sexual orientation discrimination case, the employee will likely have to answer some embarrassing questions to prove that he really is, or is not, homosexual or bisexual. Furthermore, he might declare in the lawsuit that he is gay, but then three or four years later when the case goes to trial he will be married (to a woman) or have a girlfriend, and will thus have difficulty proving that he is (or was) gay. Sexual orientation is unlike race and gender in that regard. Race and gender remain the same and are obvious to everyone. Sexual orientation can change, and is rarely obvious.

Thus, the employer's defense in a sexual orientation discrimination suit is often, "I had no idea he was gay. I fired him because of his poor job performance, not his sexual orientation. I didn't know what his sexual orientation was." If the employer is telling the truth, it will be very difficult for the employee to win the suit. If the employee never clearly indicated to the employer that the employee is gay, lesbian, or bisexual, the employee will have difficulty proving that the employer "knew" or "perceived" the employee to be gay, lesbian, or bisexual. If the employer did not know or perceive it, the employer could not have discriminated against the employee on the basis of it.

For that reason, diversity training pertaining to sexual orientation is inadvisable. That type of diversity training makes almost everyone feel uncomfortable. It generates discussion about a topic that most people have strong feelings about but would rather not discuss in the workplace. Indeed, most people have strong *negative* feelings about the topic, and those negative feelings, if expressed, can be used against them and against the company in court. The more interest and curiosity you show in an employee's sexual orientation (some trainers urge managers to show such interest in their employees), the more legal trouble you potentially bring upon yourself and your company or organization. A gay, lesbian, or bisexual employee will likely accuse you of prying into his or her love life because you are "homophobic" and you are trying to "get rid of" homosexual employees. With some of these trainers, it is unclear what their agenda is. If their agenda is to try to get you to "approve of" homosexuality, remember that the law does not require you to "approve of" homosexuality. The law (in thirteen states) requires you to *ignore* the homosexuality (if any) of your employees. Whether you "approve of" homosexuality is entirely up to you.

Post All Required Notices

Federal and state employment laws require employers to display certain posters telling employees what their rights are. Make sure you display all such posters—properly. Failure to display them can be used against you in court.

Chapter Five
Ending Discriminatory Language

"By your words you will be justified, and by your words you will be condemned." Matthew 12:37

Eliminate from your vocabulary, especially your workplace vocabulary, all offensive words that pertain to race, color, ancestry, national origin, gender, pregnancy, religion, old age, physical or mental disability, and sexual orientation. If a jury hears that you uttered discriminatory slurs, the jurors might conclude that you committed employment discrimination even if you did not.

A parable illustrates the point:

The Parable of the Latino Factory Worker

A Latino male (we'll refer to him as "the client") went to a lawyer complaining that the client's boss, Mr. X—a gruff, white, semi-educated factory owner—referred to Latinos as "spics" and fired him for being late too often. Although the client was indeed late too often, he wanted to sue for race discrimination. He felt that if a white employee had been late that often, Mr. X would have given the white employee one more chance to improve his punctuality, and not have fired him.

The lawyer asked the client how many of Mr. X's one hundred employees were Latino. The client's reply was fifty. The lawyer advised the client that he (the client) might have a good race discrimination case, and suggested in passing that he go to work for the competing factory about a mile away.

The competing factory was owned by Mr. Y, a dignified white man with an Ivy League education who is on many civic boards, goes to church every Sunday, and never utters a slur of any type. The client's reply to the lawyer's suggestion was, "I don't think I can get a job there. Mr. Y does not hire Latinos. He does not like Latinos. So I want to sue Mr. X to get my job back."

Who's the bigot, Mr. X or Mr. Y? Ordinarily, *actions* speak louder than *words*. Mr. X's *actions* show him to be an equal opportunity employer—he has many Latino employees. Mr. Y has none (or he has a few "tokens" just to avoid being accused of having an all-white workforce). Mr. Y is the bigot.

But who does the client wish to sue? Mr. X! Why? Because Mr. X calls Latinos "spics." He does not wish to sue Mr. Y even though Mr. Y is more bigoted than Mr. X. In employment discrimination law, *words* often speak louder than *actions*.

Mr. Y will probably get sued eventually. An employer should not try to avoid discrimination suits by simply refusing to hire women, people of color, older workers, and disabled workers. That is illegal. But that isn't the point here. The point here is that some of the most fair-minded employers—the ones who hire the most women and people of color—end up getting sued because they make *offensive, discriminatory remarks*. Don't make such remarks! Discriminatory remarks can get an employer into trouble even if the employer has a good or even excellent record of hiring minority workers.

Remember also that some people who would never utter a discriminatory slur under ordinary circumstances might do so in *extra*ordinary circumstances, such as when they are *extremely agitated*. Maybe you are one of them. We occasionally hear of a white football player getting angry on the field over a rough play and yelling a racial epithet at an opponent, a man of color. This happens in the workplace as well: A white manager will yell a racial slur in a heated argument with a black subordinate. Or a young manager will call an older worker an "old" this or that. Or a male manager will call a female employee a "bitch" or other gender slur. Make a conscious effort to "catch yourself" when you're angry, so you do not utter such slurs.

And don't allow any *other* employees of yours—even your lowest-level employees—to make such remarks in the workplace. Such remarks create what the law calls a "hostile work environment."

We considered making a list of all these discriminatory slurs, or as many as we could think of, and including the list in this book so you would know all the words to avoid. Believe it or not, some people do not know that all these words are offensive. They need to be told. But the list was too offensive to put in the book. So the book leaves out the *really* bad words and mentions a few that you might not realize can get you into legal trouble.

Never refer to an employee as "crazy," "nuts," "wacko," "paranoid," or "schizoid," even if he or she is. Discrimination against an employee because of mental disability can sometimes land you in legal trouble; so can *harassment* because of mental disability (or physical disability). You can talk to your fellow managers about, or discipline or discharge an employee for, the employee's poor *behavior* or poor *job performance*, but do so using nondiagnostic language. Don't "diagnose" the employee yourself unless you are a psychiatrist. If you suspect that the employee is mentally unfit, you may have the right to ask the employee to submit to a mental examination.[44] You may, depending on how bad the employee's behavior or job performance is, have the right to terminate the employee without a mental examination. But don't play psychiatrist. If anyone is going to make a mental diagnosis, let it be a psychiatrist or other qualified mental examiner.

Never, ever, tell an employee that he or she is "too old." Don't even tell someone else that an employee is "too old." Don't say "old fart," "old fogey," "old geezer," "geezer," or any other words meaning or implying old age. Don't say "We need younger people around here" or "We need new blood in this department." If you need personnel changes in a department, say "We need personnel changes in this department." You can terminate older employees just as you can terminate younger employees. But don't do it just *because* they are old, and certainly *don't tell them* they are old. Don't ever say "He's a good young marketing manager." An older worker will take offense at that, might make a note of it, and use it against you someday in an age discrimination suit.

Don't refer to any racial, ethnic, or religious group as "you people." Don't say *"you women!"* or *"you men!"* In other words, don't lump people together just because they belong to a particular racial, ethnic, religious, or gender group. If a Jewish employee orders a ham sandwich for lunch, don't say, "I thought Jews don't eat pork." Some Jews do; others don't. Don't talk about an employee's religion unless the employee brings it up, in which case you should still try to politely stay away from the topic (except that you may need to discuss it if the employee is asking for some type of religious accommodation, such as leaving by 5:00 on Fridays, not working Sundays, etc.).

If you are a man, don't refer to a female over the age of eighteen as a "girl." She is a "woman." Don't say "the girls in the office." Say "the women in the office" or, better yet, "the people in the office." Don't say "PMS," "that time of the month again," or any other words or phrases pertaining to menstruation.

If you are a woman, particularly a woman supervisor, don't say things that might lead a man to sue for sex discrimination. For example, don't say "It's their male culture" or "That's a guy thing" or "There's too much testosterone in this department."

If you work in one of the thirteen states in which discrimination against gays, lesbians, and bisexuals is illegal, don't say "homo," "queer," "faggot," or any other derogatory word about homosexuality. (Of course, you should not say those words even if you work in one of the other thirty-seven states.) Don't talk about homosexuality at all.

Language that is particularly offensive to members of a certain race, color, national origin, gender, religion, age (especially if over forty), physical or mental disability, or sexual orientation can get you into legal trouble. It can and will be used against you in court if an employee ever sues you for discrimination. It may even be the basis for the suit. It may be the only evidence the employee has. But it may be enough for the employee to win.

Have a Written Policy Prohibiting Discriminatory Slurs and Discriminatory Harassment, and Distribute It to All Employees

It is a good idea for employers to have a written policy distributed to employees that prohibits harassment, slurs, and other adverse behavior based on race, color, national origin, ancestry, sex, sexual orientation, pregnancy, age, religion, and disability. The policy will inform all your employees what type of behavior is unacceptable. Having such a policy might shield your company or organization from liability for *punitive* damages if your company or organization is ever held liable for discrimination or harassment.[45] In some cases, it might shield your company or organization from liability altogether.

Conclusion

When the Only Color Is Green

Discrimination is illegal, immoral, abusive, and should end. Employers should not discriminate on the basis of race, color, gender, age, national origin, religion, or disability. In states that prohibit discrimination on the basis of sexual orientation, employers should not discriminate on that basis, either.

Employers should not stereotype their employees. Employers should not make assumptions about men, women, whites, blacks, Latinos, Asians, Muslims, older workers, gays, and disabled workers based on what *some* men, women, whites, blacks, Latinos, Asians, Muslims, older workers, gays, and disabled workers do. Employers should not lump people together just because they are the same race, color, national origin, gender, religion, age, sexual orientation, or have the same disability. Employers should treat each person as an *individual* who may be very different from others of his or her race, color, national origin, gender, religion, age, sexual orientation, or disability group.

But some employers will continue to discriminate anyway. It is difficult to "cure" them of it because they don't think they are "sick." Many employers who discriminate do not even realize they discriminate. They claim, and they honestly believe, that the only "color" they see is "green"—money. They claim that all their decisions are based on "the bottom line." If they fire someone, they claim it is because firing that person will somehow improve "the bottom line." "I don't care if an employee is black, white, brown, red, blue, male, female, young, or old," they claim. "All I care about is how well they perform." That is what employers tell judges and juries when employers go to court to defend against discrimination lawsuits. Many of these employers are lying. But many others are telling the truth. It is difficult to know who is lying and who is telling the truth. That is why so many employees lose these suits. The burden of proof in court is usually on the plaintiff, not the defendant. The plaintiff in an employment discrimination suit is the emplo*yee*, not the emplo*yer*. If the employee cannot prove the employer is lying, the employee usually loses.

Years ago it was easier for employees to win these suits. Employers made more racist, sexist, and "ageist" (pertaining to old age) remarks back then. "We don't hire blacks." "A woman can't do this job." "You're too old for this job." "Irish need not apply." Employers would make these remarks, and these remarks would be used against them in court to prove discrimination. Those employers would lose in court.

But few employers make such remarks today. Employers who discriminate against blacks, women, and older workers today usually do so quietly. Discrimination is more subtle today. It is harder to prove discrimination today.

Thus, not only is it difficult to "cure" employers who discriminate today, it is difficult to "catch" them and bring them to justice.

As we said, however, many employers who claim their decisions are based on "the bottom line" rather than on discriminatory factors *really are* telling the truth. According to syndicated career-advice columnist Joyce Lain Kennedy, most layoff decisions are based on "who earns their keep and who doesn't."[46] "The key determinant of who survives layoffs is each employee's input to profit potential, based on his or her previous impact on bottom-line issues," she says.[47] Occasionally a layoff decision is based on gender, age, race, or other discriminatory factors, she says, but most are based on "who earns their keep and who doesn't."

A layoff decision based on "who earns their keep and who doesn't" is acceptable, according to the Bible. "He who sows sparingly will also reap sparingly; and he who sows bountifully will also reap bountifully" (2 Cor 9:6). So it is difficult to criticize employers for basing decisions on "the bottom line." The bottom line should not be their *only* consideration, of course. Employers should also consider the economic and ecological effects of their operations and the good of all persons involved (*Catechism*, par. 2432). But basing decisions on the bottom line is good in this sense: It means, hopefully, that the employer is *not* basing decisions on race, gender, age, or other discriminatory factors.

We noted that some employers who think they don't discriminate really do discriminate. Yet we also noted that some employ*ees* who think they are *victims* of discrimination really are not. Many employees (and many other types of people) tend to blame their problems on "circumstances beyond their control," such as their race, gender, or age. "I got fired. It must be because of my age." "My boss doesn't like me. It must be because I'm a woman." "I'm eighty pounds overweight. It must be that I have a low metabolism or a genetic predisposition toward being fat." "I'm an alcoholic. It must be because my father drank a lot." Some of these people are correct, but others are not. Others *assume* their problems are due to their gender, age, race, or other "circumstances beyond their control," but they are mistaken. Their problems are really due to their *inability, bad habits, lack of self-discipline,* and *difficult personalities.* These people can change and improve if they really try to, but they don't really try to. They accept little or no responsibility for their own predicaments. They don't try to correct their own faults. They blame *others.* Or they blame "circumstances beyond their control," such as their race, gender, or age. An employee who does not get along with her boss might blame it on the boss's being of a different race, gender, or age than she is. Those are "circumstances beyond her control." But in fact, the problem might be *her own* attitude, inability, poor work habits, or lack of self-discipline. Those are circumstances *within* her control.

Of course, it is also possible that the problem really is the boss's fault and not her fault. But that does not necessarily mean the boss is discriminating. It may mean that the boss has some problem himself—personality, attitude, stupidity, or whatever—but not in regard to race, gender, or age. So a discrimination lawsuit will not end the problem.

This phenomenon—blaming circumstances *beyond* one's control rather than factors *within* one's control—is exemplified by the job hunter who has a pimple on his forehead. He goes on three interviews but no one hires him. No one tells him *why* he is not hired, but he assumes it is because he looks a little funny with a pimple on his forehead. That is not necessarily the reason, though. The real reason may be that he didn't interview well or he interviewed well but not as well as the successful applicant did, or his résumé wasn't quite as good as the successful applicant's. He really doesn't know. Maybe he should try to get rid of the pimple, but he shouldn't dwell too much on the pimple. He should try to improve his résumé and interview skills, and not draw conclusions after only three interviews. Maybe the pimple had something to do with it, maybe it didn't. Maybe the pimple had something to do with one job rejection but not the other two.

He might also wish to ask one of the interviewers why he didn't get the job. It is possible the interviewer will not tell him the reason, but it is also possible the interviewer will tell him the reason. The rejected applicant will never know unless he asks. This is also true of an employee who gets fired or is about to be fired. Rather than assume it is because of race, age, gender, or handicap, he or she might wish to speak to the boss and ask the boss what the problem is. Making assumptions rather than speaking face to face with the boss is like choosing darkness over light. Speaking to the boss will not necessarily yield the entire truth, for maybe the boss really is discriminating on the basis of race, age, gender, or handicap—and will try to hide the truth. But maybe *some* light will come from the conversation. There is at least *some* chance that the employee will learn to see herself as others see her. As St. Paul said, "For now we see in a mirror, dimly, but then face to face. Now I know in part; but then I shall know just as I also am known" (1 Cor 13:12).

Knowing oneself as one is known by others is a key to career success. People who feel they were fired or not hired because of their race, gender, age, or other discriminatory reason should be open to the possibility that that was *not* the reason. Maybe it was, maybe it wasn't. As we noted, years ago many employees did not have to *wonder* whether they were victims of discrimination. They *knew* they were victims of discrimination. They would apply for a job and be told, "No Negroes." A pregnant woman would get fired from a job and be told, "A pregnant woman can't do this job." But as we noted, those days are largely gone. Few employers say those things today. Today a black employee who gets fired after fifteen years on the job and feels he is a victim of race discrimination might have difficulty proving that race had anything to do with the firing. His boss probably did not make a racist remark or otherwise display prejudice against blacks. The boss will defend against the suit by saying, "You were black when I hired you. You were black the entire fifteen years you worked here. If I were prejudiced against blacks, I would not have hired you. Or I would have fired you a long time ago. So obviously I am not prejudiced against blacks. I fired you for reasons other than your race, namely, your poor job performance and poor attitude. You should try to improve your job performance and attitude." As blunt and simplistic as the boss sounds, he may be telling the truth. The employee's job performance and attitude really may have been poor. It may be that a white employee with the same poor job performance and attitude would have been fired, too. If a white employee with the same poor job performance and attitude would have been fired, there was no discrimination. The black employee was treated exactly the way the white employee would have been.

That is why it is often difficult for an employee who worked for an employer for many years to sue the employer for race discrimination, gender discrimination, religion discrimination, or national origin discrimination. The employer hired that employee and kept that employee on the payroll for many years even though that employee was of that race, gender, religion, and national origin. It is difficult to accuse the employer of suddenly discriminating against that employee due to race, gender, religion, or national origin.

That is the sad irony of employment discrimination law. Most of the suits are initiated by people who were fired, not by rejected job applicants. Yet the people who were fired usually aren't the ones who were discriminated against, so most of them either lose or receive very little money in the suit.[48] The rejected job applicants—the people who weren't hired to begin with—are more likely to be the ones who were discriminated against. Yet they rarely sue. We discussed this in chapter 5 ("The parable of the Latino factory worker"). Whatever the reason for this irony, it proves the underlying thesis of this book: Ending discrimination in the workplace requires effort by employers *and* employees. Just suing, threatening, lecturing, and cajoling the employers won't end it.

Perhaps the best tip we can give employees to end discrimination in the workplace is to be the best employee you can be. The best employees are discriminated against far less than the mediocre employees are. Most employers don't want to do anything to offend or lose the best employees. They want to keep the best employees. Most employers really do care more about "green" than any other color.

Then again, caring *too* much about "green" can lead to trouble, too. The Bible disapproves of employers who earn huge profits from their employees' labor and live extravagantly but pay their employees poorly. That is not discrimination, however. It is greed. This book is about discrimination, not greed. But greed is relevant to discrimination in this respect: Employers who live extravagantly are probably more likely to get *sued* for discrimination (not necessarily more likely to *lose* a discrimination suit, but more likely to get sued in the first place) than employers who don't. Many fired employees sue their employer not because they really believe their employer discriminated or otherwise violated the law but because they are angry and need money. They resent their employer's living extravagantly off the employee's labor and then dumping the employee onto the street. They want the employer to "share the wealth" more by paying the employee a settlement package or jury verdict. An employee who is earning a modest hourly wage and gets fired might sue the employer for discrimination (we noted in the introduction that most lawsuits by employees against employers are discrimination suits) and seek hundreds of thousands of dollars in damages. The employer will react as though the employee is some kind of thief trying to steal the employer's money. The employee has no right to the money, argues the employer. But even if the employer is correct—even if the suit has no basis—the employer should recall the words of Jesus: "Do not lay up for yourselves treasures on earth, where moths and rust destroy and where thieves break in and steal" (Matt 6:19). The more "treasure" the employer shows off, the more likely a disgruntled employee will try to "steal" it.

Many employers will no doubt respond, "I earned my money honestly. I worked very hard for it, harder than most of my employees work. I took risks they did not take. I am entitled to live in luxury. My employees are not entitled to sue me unless I violated their rights. I have not violated their rights." Even if these employers are correct, the fact remains that if they lived more modestly, fewer employees would sue them. Much litigation in this country is simply an effort by poor and modest-means people to redistribute wealth by suing the rich. Employers, especially large employers, are often referred to as "deep pockets" in legal jargon. Poor and modest-means plaintiffs try to get their hands into the "deep pockets" of employers, insurance companies, the government, and other "well-heeled" entities. So, one way employers can reduce the number of discrimination lawsuits is to live less extravagantly.

Of course, not every employer is rich and not every employer lives extravagantly. Employees should keep that in mind. Employees who feel like victims of discrimination should realize that employers often feel like victims, too. Employers feel like victims when employees do not try their hardest; when employees make mistakes that cause their employers to lose money and customers; when employees fail, for whatever reason, to generate enough revenue for their employer to pay their salaries; and when employees learn their employer's business and then go to work for a competitor of their employer. Employees should keep in mind that eight out of ten businesses fail. These failures cause financial losses, and sometimes great financial hardship, to the owners. Even employers who accumulate some wealth sometimes lose that wealth quickly when times get tough. Paying employees during hard times can drain hundreds of thousands of dollars, or even millions of dollars, from an employer in a short period of time.

That is why most employees never try to become employers themselves. They know it is financially risky. They know eight out of ten fail. It is a good thing that some people try to be employers, because if no one did, there would be no jobs.

Saints and Jobs

The risks of being an employer—particularly the risk of starting a business and hiring an employee to begin with—are no doubt what St. Peter had in mind when he said, "Servants, be submissive to your masters with all fear, not only to the good and gentle, but also to the harsh" (1 Pet 2:18). Even a harsh employer deserves credit for one thing: He or she gives people jobs. He or she provides people with a living. If the people who complain about "harsh" employers had to meet a payroll themselves, they would probably be harsh, too.

It is true that most employers are not "saints." But it is also true that most "saints" are not employers. Most "saints"—that is, nice people such as schoolteachers, social workers, nurses, the clergy, and others who go around doing good deeds and are never accused of being "harsh" or "cheap" like employers are—do not provide many jobs. They do not pay people much money. People need money to buy food, clothing, shelter, and the other necessities and amenities of life. They receive most of that money from "harsh," "cheap" employers, not from "saints." That is basically what St. Peter was telling us: We need "saints," but we also need employers. It is difficult to be both.

St. Paul, too, recognized the need for employers and jobs. Paul said to Titus, "Exhort servants to be obedient to their own masters, to be well pleasing in all things, not answering back, not pilfering, but showing all good fidelity" (Titus 2:9–10). Paul wanted to reward people for taking the risks necessary to become employers and provide jobs. Paul did not want to reward employers *too* much, however. He did not want power to go to their heads. So he admonished them, "Masters, give your servants what is just and fair, knowing that you also have a Master in heaven" (Col 4:1).

So it all boils down to this: Employers should not discriminate, but at the same time, employees should not be too quick to see themselves as "victims." In many cases, only God knows who the true "victim" is.

Endnotes

1. Women currently make up 12.5 percent of corporate officers and represent just 4.1 percent of all top earners. *Working Woman*, April 2001, p. 6. African Americans hold 8.2 percent of executive slots, and Hispanics 5 percent (ibid.). Only five Fortune 500 companies have a woman CEO. Claudia H. Deutsch, "Xerox Moves Up an Insider to Be Its Chief," *New York Times*, July 27, 2001, p. C4.

2. "Job discrimination cases remain one of the single most unsuccessful classes of litigation for plaintiffs," according to Cornell University law professor Theodore Eisenberg, quoted in "Suppose They Sue?" *U.S. News & World Report*, September 22, 1997, p. 69. "They settle less and lose more than almost anything else," said Eisenberg. See also "Suspect Age Bias? Try Proving It," *Fortune*, February 1, 1999, p. 58 ("Even if an employee manages to take his case to court, it's unlikely he will win"). According to *HR* magazine (published by the Society for Human Resources Management), December 1996 (p. 8), "The majority of middle-aged and older women who seek legal recourse for age and sex bias do not prevail in court." As far as Americans with Disabilities Act cases, the *ABA* (American Bar Association) *Journal* reported in April 1999 (p. 34) that "Plaintiffs have lost in the trial court in 94 percent of ADA cases." Even if an employee wins a large jury verdict, large jury verdicts in job discrimination cases are more likely to be reversed or reduced than in any other type of litigation, according to "Judges Slash Worker Awards," *National Law Journal*, April 20, 1998, p. A1.

3. The extent to which church and state are, or should be, separate in this country is a matter of endless debate. The Constitution does not use the word "separate," nor does it say there shall be a "wall" between church and state. Those terms are used by people who interpret the Constitution that way. But the Constitution does not say that. It says this: "Congress shall make no law respecting an establishment of religion, or prohibiting the free exercise thereof." The U.S. Supreme Court has held that this applies not only to Congress but also to the fifty state governments (and to municipal governments, too).

As this book goes to press, the debate over "separation of church and state" is raging anew. President Bush has proposed faith-based social welfare programs. Some people are concerned that the federal government will be funding religious activities and preferring some religions over others.

Due to the difficulty of figuring out exactly what our founding fathers meant by "shall make no law respecting an establishment of religion, or prohibiting the free exercise thereof," the extent to which "church" and "state" are "separate" will forever depend on what the American people, or a majority of them, want at a given time. The American people elect the president, and the president gets to choose who the U.S. Supreme Court judges and other federal judges will be. Those judges get to decide what the Constitution means.

4. "Ethics in the Workplace," www.pcusa.org/pcusa/today/features (March 10, 2001).

5. In some states, however, it *is* legal to have a mandatory retirement age as to certain types of jobs.

6. "Ethics in the Workplace," www.pcusa.org/pcusa/today/features (March 10, 2001).

7. This quote is not from *The Peter Principle*; however, it is something Dr. Peter said in his book *Peter's Quotations: Ideas for Our Time* (New York: Bantam, 1979), p. 441.

8. The primary federal employment discrimination law, Title VII of the Civil Rights Act of 1964, 42 U.S.C. §2000e-2(a)(1) & (2), reads as follows: "It shall be an unlawful employment practice for an employer to fail or refuse to hire or to discharge any individual, or otherwise to discriminate against any individual with respect to his compensation, terms, conditions, or privileges of employment, because of such individual's race, color, religion, sex, or national origin; or to limit, segregate, or classify his employees or applicants for employment in any way which would deprive or tend to deprive any individual of employment opportunities or otherwise adversely affect his status as an employee, because of such individual's race, color, religion, sex, or national origin."

A similar federal law pertaining to race discrimination reads, "All persons...shall have the same right...to make and enforce contracts...as is enjoyed by white citizens" (42 U.S.C. § 1981).

There are also federal laws pertaining to age and disability discrimination.

9. Genesis 1:27 is the foundation of the United Methodist Church's proclamation "Faith in Action: Overcoming Racism and Sexism":

> "Racism is the belief that one race is innately superior to all other races. This belief is the denial of the wisdom of God in creation. Scripture tells us that in the beginning all people were created in God's image thus becoming God's children, the Household of God. From this perspective of our faith racism is a sin. We recognize racism as sin and affirm the ultimate and temporal worth of all persons. We rejoice in the gifts that particular ethnic histories and cultures bring to our total life" (www.umc.org/faithinaction/racism {December 2, 2000}).

10. Abram Katz, "One Race," *New Haven Register,* October 26, 1997, p. A8.

11. www.lcms.org/president/statements/wlracism (March 10, 2001).

12. Robert F. Kennedy, "Suppose God Is Black?" *Look*, August 23, 1966, p. 45.

13. Quoted in "Catholicism's Claim to Primacy Reaffirmed by Pontiff," *Boston Globe*, October 2, 2000, p. A11.

14. "Equal Protection and Intelligence Classifications," 26 *Stanford Law Review* 647, 648, n.5 (1974) (to many blacks, IQ tests and aptitude tests "reflect the values and promote the goals of the white, middle-class establishment; their use is seen as antagonistic to the long-term interests of members of minority cultures").

15. Black students spend as much time on homework as white students do and have the same attendance rate as white students have. Philip J. Cook and Jens Ludwig, "The Burden of 'Acting White': Do Black Adolescents Disparage Academic Achievement?" in Christopher Jencks and Meredith Phillips, eds., *The Black-White Test Score Gap* (Washington, D.C.: Brookings Institution Press, 1998), p. 390 (hereinafter *The Black-White Test Score Gap*).

16. Black students tend to do more poorly on tests if they know that the sole purpose of the test is to measure their intelligence. Christopher Jencks, "Racial Bias in Testing," in *The Black-White Test Score Gap*, n. 14, p. 70. Blacks (and women) tend to distrust these tests because they believe that these tests have historically been used by

white males to perpetuate white male dominance (ibid.). Blacks are more likely to think these tests are "tricky and unfair" than whites are. Claude M. Steele and Joshua Aronson, "Stereotype Threat and the Test Performance of Academically Successful African Americans," in *The Black-White Test Score Gap*, p. 417. This causes them discomfit not only *during* the test but *the night before the test*, so they do not sleep well the night before. This further diminishes their performance on the test (ibid.). Consequently, blacks (and women, to a somewhat lesser degree) are more likely to "disengage" from these tests than whites are. Ronald F. Ferguson, "Teachers' Perceptions and Expectations and the Black-White Test Score Gap," in *The Black-White Test Score Gap*, p. 291. Blacks (and women) are more likely than whites are to decide that their performance on these tests is not important to their personal goals or self-perceptions (ibid., p. 290).

17. In Japan, by contrast, "test scores literally make or break the college aspirations of young people, rich and poor alike. Therefore, students face these examinations with the utmost seriousness, and parents often enlist the services of tutors to supplement their children's regular classroom study." John J. Macionis, *Sociology*, 2d ed. (Englewood Cliffs, N.J.: Prentice Hall, 1989), p. 402. Of course, in the United States many students and their parents also approach these tests with the utmost seriousness and enlist the aid of tutors. "In the United States, however, even students with low SAT scores can expect to be admitted to some college…" (ibid.).

18. See www.umc.org/gcrr/home (December 2, 2000).

19. *Grutter v. Bollinger*, 288 F.3d 732 (6th Cir. 2002); *Gratz v. Bollinger*, 122 F. Supp. 2d 811 (E.D. Mich. 2000).

20. "Men and Women Are Both from Earth" was a headline in the *New York Times Book Review*, April 11, 1999, p. 19. The author of this book cannot take credit for the line.

21. Cambridge: Harvard University Press, 1993 ed., p. 14.

22. *Springfield* [Mass.] *Union-News*, November 29, 2000, p. A1. The headline refers to an Indiana University School of Medicine study. The study was widely reported in newspapers and newscasts across the nation in late November and early December 2000.

23. *Springfield* [Mass.] *Union-News*, April 11, 2001, p. B1.

24. *Boston Globe*, April 19, 2001, p. A2.

25. *Springfield* [Mass.] *Union-News*, January 17, 1999, p. A8.

26. See "Faith in Action: Overcoming Racism and Sexism," www.umc.org/faithinaction/racism (December 2, 2000).

27. www.pcusa.org/women/d5 (December 2, 2000).

28. 42 U.S.C. §2000e(k).

29. June 1999, p. 32.

30. Jane Bryant Quinn, "Which Spouse Has Paycheck Power?" *Springfield* [Mass.] *Sunday Republican*, May 30, 1999, p. F3.

31. *Oncale v. Sundowner Offshore Services, Inc.*, 523 U.S. 75, 81 (1998) (the federal sexual harassment law "forbids only behavior so objectively offensive as to alter the 'conditions' of the victim's employment"). Ordinarily, simple teasing, offhand comments, and isolated incidents (unless extremely serious) do not amount to sexual harassment under federal law. *Clark County School District v. Breeden*, 121 S. Ct. 1508, 1509–10 (2001), citing *Faragher v. City of Boca Raton*, 524 U.S. 775, 788 (1998).

32. *Oncale v. Sundowner Offshore Services, Inc.*, 523 U.S. 75 (1998).

33. "Reasonable Accommodation and Undue Hardship under the Americans with Disabilities Act," *EEOC Enforcement Guidance*, Mar. 1, 1999 ("Undue Hardship Issues").

34. "Disability-Related Inquiries and Medical Examinations of Employees under the Americans with Disabilities Act," *EEOC Enforcement Guidance*, July 27, 2000.

35. 42 U.S.C. §12102(2)(A).

36. 42 U.S.C. §12102(2)(B) & 2(C).

37. See "Differently Disabled," *ABA Journal* (American Bar Association), April 1999, p. 34.

38. *Murphy v. United Parcel Service Inc.*, 527 U.S. 516 (1999); *Sutton v. United Airlines*, 527 U.S. 471 (1999); *Toyota Motor Manuf., Ky., Inc. v. Williams*, 534 U.S. 184 (2002).

39. ADA regulation 29 CFR §1630.9 (App.): "When the need for accommodation is not obvious, an employer, before providing a reasonable accommodation, may require that the individual with a disability provide documentation of the need for accommodation."

40. See *EEOC v. Wyoming*, 460 U.S. 226, 231 (1983) (pointing out that the U.S. Secretary of Labor conducted a study that found that, generally speaking, the job performance of older workers is at least as good as that of younger workers).

41. The sentence "Make it your skills that stand out—not your age" appeared in a *Boston Sunday Globe* (July 29, 2001, at H10) calendar of upcoming lectures and workshops, pertaining to a workshop for older job seekers. The author cannot take credit for that sentence.

42. www.pcusa.org/pcusa/info/homosexu (December 2, 2000).

43. It is possible that some of the laws protecting homosexuals from discrimination will be declared invalid due to the Supreme Court's decision in *Boy Scouts of America v. Dale*, 120 S. Ct. 2446 (2000). The Court held that the New Jersey branch of the *Boy Scouts* has the right to ban homosexuals from being scoutmasters even though New Jersey has a law that protects homosexuals from discrimination. The *Boy Scouts* case is not really an "employment" case, but it could conceivably be interpreted to mean that an employer who is morally opposed to homosexuality does not have to hire homosexuals.

44. Americans with Disabilities Act, 42 U.S.C. §12112(A). According to *EEOC Policy Guidance:* "The Americans with Disabilities Act and Psychiatric Disabilities" (March 25, 1997), "[M]edical examinations are permitted...if they address reasonable concerns about whether an individual is fit to perform essential functions of his/her position." Such examinations are particularly permitted when "an employer has a reasonable belief, based on objective evidence, that...an employee will pose a direct threat due to a medical condition" (ibid.).

45. See *Kolstad v. American Dental Association*, 527 U.S. 526 (1999); *EEOC Enforcement Guidance:* "Vicarious Employer Liability for Unlawful Harassment by Supervisors" (June 18, 1999).

46. Joyce Lain Kennedy, "Why Was Model Employee Laid Off?" *Springfield* (Mass.) *Sunday Republican*, June 10, 2001, p. E4, quoting Paul Hawkinson, *The Fordyce Letter* (www.Fordyceletter.com), an employment newsletter.

47. Ibid.

48. See note 2 above.

Index